To

My little town

'In this great future you can't forget your past.'

Bob Marley 1945–1981

Dedication

Long before the digital age introduced sampling to the music industry, legendary pop duo, Simon & Garfunkel performed some rudimentary sampling of their own. They borrowed a stanza from a WH Auden poem and inserted it into their own song.

Auden's lines were 'After it rains there's a rainbow/ And all of the colours are black/ It's not that the colours aren't there/ It's just *imagination* they lack'. Then, they added their own words 'I'm never going back – to my little town'.

These are words which will surely resonate with many people who grew up in little towns; towns with little aspiration; little belief; little inspiration. Places where people can quite easily resign themselves to nothingness – little by little.

So it is with this in mind that I dedicate this book to my little town, and to people in little towns everywhere. Auden was right – the colours *are* there. You have to fight to discover your imaginative powers, and when you do the only limits are the limits you place upon yourself.

Most of the people in this book started out staring at a black rainbow. Today, they are colourful characters with colourful lives. They are the entrepreneurs living on the edge.

Wherever you are, whatever you do, please fight for the right to exercise your imaginative powers. There is a colourful world out there.

Acknowledgements

Working on this book has been an absolute joy, and an inspiration to me. I feel very privileged to know so many amazing people with such incredible stories. So my first thanks go to the characters featured in this book, for their time and their stories, and of course for the business ideas that have occurred to me as I have analysed their successes and failures.

Thanks also to the people who used their powers of persuasion to get the right people in the right place, believing that I could do justice to their story. The people who 'oiled the wheels' were Selwyn Demmy, Sara Lawton, Tracey Friedel and Clare Cooper.

Meanwhile, the staff at The Bubble Room have ensured that my table by the window has been supplied with countless pots of tea during my afternoon writing sessions, and I thank them for the interest they have taken in the guy in the corner lost in his imagination day after day.

Thanks go to my editor Emma Swaisland for doing something that makes everything seem easy – she accentuated the positive, which meant that I was willing to accept her judgement when she told me the things that just didn't work.

Finally, I want to thank my friend 'The Prince'. Albert Edwards and I were born within hours of each other, little more than a mile apart. He has made me laugh a great deal, inspired me through my difficult times and over the years has said some outrageous and 'off the wall' things which have often made me see a completely different way of doing things. He is a genuine Clown Prince.

Contents

1

Don't push me ... I'm close to the edge

Think of the richest square mile in Britain, and your thoughts immediately turn to the City of London or Chelsea.

In fact, a small village in Cheshire is home to more millionaires per square mile than anywhere else in Britain. The place is Alderley Edge, a tract of lush countryside thirty miles south of Manchester. It is a place where one in twenty houses sells for more than £1 million. According to Experian, the credit agency, 20% of residents enjoy a *seven* figure income and in its index of 'poshness' Alderley Edge scored 136 out of a maximum 137.

It is also the focal point of what has been described as Britain's 'Golden Triangle', an area formed by joining the dots between the points of Wilmslow, the village of Prestbury, and the jewel in the crown, Alderley Edge itself. It is both a semi-rural extended village and a topographical landmark. The Edge is a 500 foot sandstone escarpment rising dramatically above the Cheshire plain.

The media coverage of this golden triangle tends to focus upon the glitz and the glamour, the celebrity residents and proliferation of Bentleys and Ferraris. They create an image of a shallow *noveau riche*.

But that's not the real story. In fact, the success and the wealth have been hard-earned. These are self-made people. Entrepreneurs with amazing stories – triumphs, tribulations, disasters and incredible recoveries. There is another side to Alderley Edge and the golden triangle, one that the outsider would not see, and one that the media cares not to see.

The real stories are not to be found amongst the wannabe 'Champagne Charlies' that stalk the bars and restaurants, with their ever more incredulous tales of their next big deal. The real stories are to be found in the alcoves and corner tables; from the guy with the pot of camomile tea; from the millionaire in the Marks & Spencer's jumper; from the lady that bounces into the room with her infectious laugh; from the man who looks like the quiet librarian type; and many others. Mostly, people you wouldn't look at twice. Yet these are the people with the real stories. These are the movers and shakers.

The entrepreneurial spirit is concentrated in these streets like nowhere else in Britain. There is a richness of experience, talent, acumen, attitude, enterprise,

1

tenacity and grittiness which, if you could bottle it, would be an immensely power-ful source of guidance and inspiration for any would-be entrepreneur.

To the Edge bottles the essence of the self-made entrepreneur and enterpriser, by looking where nobody has bothered to look before: into the lives and the busi-ness highs and lows of the people who inhabit the streets, the lanes, the alcoves and the corner tables of this extraordinary place.

It goes deeper than many other examinations of entrepreneurs, which often focus more on the froth than the Guinness. We are going to drill down beyond the froth to find out where these people came from, what drove them to their success-es, what sustained them during their failures, and to look at what can be learned from their beliefs, behaviours and often quite exceptional experiences.

If you are a business person, entrepreneur or business owner needing a shot of inspiration, then this book is for you. If you are in need of some sharp insights into what it takes to become seriously rich and successful, then this book is for you. If you are simply an observer of human nature and want to be inspired by some quite incredible stories of the power of people to overcome whatever obstacles are placed in their way, then this book is for you.

You will find that the nature of entrepreneurs is to always be pushing back the boundaries, trying new things, blurring the edges. They thrive when they live life on the edge. **For these people, they feel that if they are not living on the edge they are taking up too much room.**

So if you want to glimpse the powerful secrets of entrepreneurial success, get ready; if you want to gain real insight into the extraordinary attitudes and behav-iours of a group of extraordinary people, get ready; if you want to look beyond the media hype and behind what makes these people really tick, then get ready.

Get ready, because I am going to take you closer, closer than you have ever been to some of the least known, most colourful entrepreneurs in Britain. I'm going to take you closer … closer to The Edge.

Not quite Camelot – more Meritopolis

According to legend, Alderley Edge is the home of the Wizard Merlin, the sor-cerer in the court of King Arthur. He is the custodian of the King and his Knights of the Round Table, who await in suspended animation in the caves on the edge, for a time when England needs their help.

The thirteen Knights of the Round Table were the extraordinary people of their day. They were chosen because of their acts of bravery and chivalry and their extraordinary ability to consistently follow their values and beliefs in the face of adversity.

In that sense, they were just like entrepreneurs, and if there were a court of King Arthur today, it would no doubt be formed of the kinds of people whose stories I will reveal in this book.

Thirteen of them. The latter-day Knights of the Round Table perhaps?

Each with a different style, a different story. Each committed wholeheartedly, unequivocally, to the path that they have chosen.

Though Alderley Edge is not quite Camelot – a magical place and the bastion of chivalry – it does have its own kind of magic. A quiet kind of magic, where extraordinary men and women win against the odds and live in a kind of meritocracy, where their standing and influence is based not on where they came from or which school they went to, but on what they have done. **It is a miniature Meritopolis. The kind of place that politicians say they want Britain to become.**

So why does so much flak come in the direction of The Edge and the Golden Triangle?

If we really want a nation built on merit, a classless society, we should rejoice. Yet so often the media choose to focus on style over substance, froth over fact, gossip over greatness.

My daughter told me that at school there is a wallchart which describes a range of careers and the attributes required. Against the section on entrepreneurs, the attribute stated is 'Selfish'. I have found this to be a ridiculous and off-beam generalization. Certainly entrepreneurs are highly focused on achieving their objectives, they can be incisive, they can make unpopular decisions. But that's business. It's not personal. It doesn't mean that they are selfish, and it is time to dispel this media-perpetuated myth that entrepreneurs are self-interested in a vaguely villainous way.

I have found the cross section of entrepreneurs featured in this book, between them, to possess all of the characteristics that make life worth living: innate goodness; kindness; compassion; philanthropy; chivalry; humour; social awareness, humility and an affinity with the underdog.

Perhaps in an odd sort of way, it is time to begin to appreciate entrepreneurs and celebrate what they stand for, to embrace this Meritopolis that is the Golden Triangle, and to learn the lessons that will stand us in good stead for dealing with the opportunities of today and tomorrow – a new kind of Camelot.

Creative communities

In small pockets around the world, creative communities have sprung up almost spontaneously. Nashville, USA is one such place: a small geographical area with a common interest – country music. It comprises established stars; backing musicians; wannabes; prospects; and inevitably fantasists. The same mix of char-

3

acters could be found in other creative communities: from Findhorn, the spiritual community in Scotland, to Silicon Valley in California, movers, shakers, fantasists, wannabes and supporting cast seem to be common characteristics.

In that sense Alderley Edge could be seen as a creative community for entrepreneurs – a place where ideas mix together, where boundaries get blurred, where people have the confidence to try new things. This idea first dawned upon me one wet Tuesday evening whilst I was sitting with a small group of friends in The Alderley Bar & Grill. Another couple of people joined our group and then some others, so that we had to pull two tables together. The older guys were regaling each other with stories of their business highs and lows, whilst the younger ones laughed and talked about their plans. Then I did something simple. I sat back and leaned my chair back onto its legs. This small movement distanced me from what was going on. These may be my everyday surroundings, I thought, but as I looked at who was around the table and considered what each of the people had done, I realized it was a quite extraordinary situation. **Living in Alderley Edge is like having a masterclass at Harvard Business School, every time you go out for a cup of coffee.** If only you could bottle that knowledge and experience, I thought. This book is my attempt to do the bottling and the distilling, to capture the essence of this creative community of entrepreneurs and make it available to others. It was one of those small insights – one which I hope will make a big difference to the thousands of people across the world who read this book.

The engine of this creative community tends not to be those who shout loudest, but those who go quietly about their business.

In the chapters that follow, we are going to meet some quite remarkable people:

- **The Alchemist** has an amazing knack of turning business base metal into gold, by buying companies for a pound and transforming their fortunes. His new store has been voted one of the 100 most inspirational stores in the world. He says he thought about the concept over a couple of pints. Whatever it is the Alchemist is drinking it certainly hits the spot.

- **The Soapstar** cut his teeth as an actor in an Australian soap and headed for the UK to become a star. Whilst waiting for his big break he worked as a cocktail waiter and forgot all about acting as he became captivated by the restaurant business. Today, his group owns 34 restaurants, turns over more than £50 million a year, and is growing at an incredible rate.

- **The Rover** is at the top of his profession. One that has hardly changed at all since its roots in the late nineteenth century. He cannot hot desk or log in from home. To do his job he has to be there. It has been good to him. He has earned enough money never to have to work again. Yet he will always work. He has found within himself an enterprising nature and a genuine desire to help people. He is showing how making money and doing good need not be mutually exclusive, they can be symbiotic.

- **The Hustler** took possession of his bus pass nearly a decade ago. He has sold three businesses for more than £50 million at today's prices, yet he still goes to work seven days a week. At the age of 74, he has had more comebacks than Frank Sinatra. Who knows where the story will end?

- **The Undertaker** has an insatiable work ethic. When he combined this with his ability to decide what was important and focus upon it, he became the top life policy salesman in the whole of Europe at just twenty-three years old. He created his own product which has boomed as more and more Britons have taken up residence overseas. It's a fantastic business. People pay up front and nobody really wants to make a claim.

- **The Prince** stared into the darkness of the 500 foot sandstone escarpment that is Alderley Edge. His business troubles weighed heavily on his shoulders and he wondered as he stared into the abyss, 'Is this the way out?'. He looked across at the distant lights of the city where as a boy he had dreamed of glory. There was a way out. This was not it. He decided at that moment that in life and in business you should never, ever, ever, ever give up. Ever. Today he takes on property projects that are too messy or too risky for traditional developers. He has an extraordinary resilience towards risk. Whatever the difficulties, he refuses to give up.

- **The Hippies** lived in a commune, married in kaftans and have been driven by passion ever since they can remember. They set up a childcare business which today turns over £30 million. Yet to them, this is nothing more than an incidental statistic in their story. It was never about the money. It was about love, passion, creativity, people, music, poetry and togetherness. It was about breaking with the established way of doing things.

- **The Maverick** says he is not very good at anything, except, that is, for his amazing ability to get on with people. It's been a useful skill as he created success as an entrepreneur and then lost everything; brought his maverick style to bear on a business within a plc, turning it around from being the worst performer to the best in just three years; and now, back in business as an entrepreneur, he went from nothing to £175 million in little more than nine months.

- **The Magic Bean** is an ethical entrepreneur who gives her staff more than just luncheon vouchers. They have group psychotherapy, a life coach and their own personal development budget which they can spend on anything that they believe will make them a better person and a more ethical professional. She likes to make money and knows how to do it. She demands to be paid handsomely for a job done amazingly. Then she gives a lot of her money away. She earns from the rich to give to the poor.

- **The Carer** screamed as she looked at the reddened mess where she had slashed the razor across her wrists. Fortunately this was not to be her end. Neither was it to be her beginning. Her turning point in life came much later, but only after she had endured physical abuse; become a teenage mum twice; tried to take her own life; had a financial fallout with her mother and her husband; and lost the love of her life in a tragic accident. Remarkably, unbelievably, not only has she survived, she is the charismatic owner of a business which is attracting the attention of serious buyers and as of today is valued for sale at £8 million.

- **The Bubbleboy** is barely out of nappies in business terms. He started his first venture at the tender age of twenty, and surpassed everyone's expectations, including his own. His business plans were hopelessly, stupendously off beam; so much so that he was delighted when he had to tear them up. He has learned something that you will never learn at business school: you have to pass the elbow test.

- **The Thinker** bought a book at the age of eight and found that it contained the foundations for creating a life that he can love. He practises the art of living on thin air. Mostly, his products cannot be seen, measured or weighed. He is in the business of creating and selling insight, using principles that have more in common with TV chef Delia Smith than with those laid down by the economist Adam Smith. In the new economy, knowledge and insight are becoming the new currency. It is worth watching the way the Thinker works: his insights contain the keys to something we are all looking for – a life that we can love.

So, here are thirteen people who can, in their different ways, offer you insights and inspiration. Meaningful insights which you can use to change the way you think, the way you work, the way you live and perhaps help you to become more entrepreneurial yourself. Unlike other books on entrepreneurs this is not a sanitized account of success. **These are not untouchable superheroes; these are real people.** Between them, they have had trials, tribulations, trauma; they have won and lost, bounced back, and changed tack. There is as much learning to be had in their mistakes and misjudgements as there is in their successes.

So why choose these thirteen people? There are other people around the Golden Triangle who may merit a mention. Some may have more wealth, others a higher profile. In the end, the choice of subjects was based upon some simple criteria. It was not about how much money people have accumulated, though you will see that some have done rather well on that score. It was about who could offer real insights; who would unfold an interesting story; and who was accessible. I determined accessibility on the basis that people should be one, or at the most two, phone calls away from me.

What has emerged is a magnificent cross section of people with great stories from a wide range of businesses. You will see that they could not have been more honest and more open. It will provide some tremendous insights which you can draw upon in your surge towards success as well as in your darkest hours. And when you do have dark days, don't be discouraged: many of the people featured in this book have had dark days too.

Inside the mind of a millionaire

Just what is it that goes on inside the minds of entrepreneurial people that makes them so different, that gives them the ability to achieve extraordinary things, that drives them through almost any obstacle?

Far from being a fanciful thought, thanks to the work of Dr Adrian Atkinson, a psychologist with whom I have become good friends, we are now able to see inside the mind of an entrepreneur.

In June 2004 the BBC commissioned a television series, *Mind of a Millionaire*. They selected thirty people to take part at Adrian's HQ, Edstone Hall in Warwickshire. Of the thirty people, fifteen of them were successful millionaire entrepreneurs and fifteen were not. The expert panel, of which Adrian was a member, were asked to try to work out who were the entrepreneurs and who were not.

Using a fifteen-minute questionnaire that he has devised, based on fifteen years of research, Adrian correctly identified fourteen of the fifteen entrepreneurs. What was he seeing? Why is the mind of an entrepreneur different and what can we learn from it?

The tool he uses to diagnose what type of mind people have is called the Personal Enterprise Profile (PEP). It puts people into a particular mindset based on their responses to the questionnaire, and, according to Adrian, has been shown to be 95% accurate. Here's an example of the output from a PEP test, one completed by a serial entrepreneur, somebody who creates one business after another:

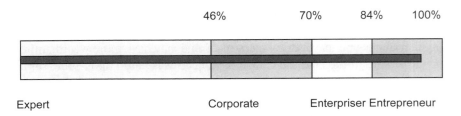

The dark bar indicates that this person's score was well into the 90th percentile and therefore into the zone of the entrepreneur. You will see that there are in fact four mindsets: Expert; Corporate; Enterpriser; and Entrepreneur.

Enterprisers and entrepreneurs are the people who create businesses by taking personal risk. There are a number of differences between the two, largely regarding the level of personal risks that each is prepared to take and the scale of the businesses that they create. The entrepreneur takes bigger risks and produces businesses on a bigger scale. Interestingly though, enterprisers tend to be more intelligent than entrepreneurs and are more capable of working with other people.

We need enterprisers and entrepreneurs. These people revitalize the economy and create new markets, an essential role when the average European business will fizzle out after twenty-six years. Yet they are quite rare. In the male population about 9% will be enterprisers and only 5% will be at the entrepreneur end of the scale. In the female population they are even more scarce, the figures being 2% and 1% respectively.

The scarcity of women entrepreneurs is reflected in the cross section of people featured in this book. They are hard to come by. One study has suggested that if we in the UK could encourage female entrepreneurs and enterprisers at the same rate as the USA, we would benefit from having an extra 700,000 businesses in the economy. At that rate, unemployment would be all but eradicated.

It is worth taking a brief look at all four types of mindset that the PEP identifies.

Expert

These people are highly accomplished in their specialist field. They tend to have an intrinsic fascination with their area of expertise rather than any potential for its commercial exploitation. They are highly risk averse and tend to be most comfortable in situations where they can focus their energies towards their specialist subject with like-minded people. These would be, for example, scientists, engineers and inventors. They can produce great products and inventions, but they will never be able to exploit their commercial potential without some enterprising help.

Corporate

These people need the strength and security of an organization around them. At the extreme end of this scale are the high-achieving corporate captains of industry who can become extremely successful and wealthy – but they are at their best when they are taking calculated risks with the resources of the organization.

Enterpriser

The enterpriser may work on their own account, running their own business perhaps, or may be found pushing back the boundaries in corporate organizations. Invariably they are very bright, though not necessarily academically qualified; they are excellent critical thinkers; they can analyse situations quickly and intelligently; and they have the ability to see things strategically.

They are driven by their need for achievement, control, status and dominance and are in search of fast, significant progress. They want to be at the top of the league in whatever it is that they do.

They do take personal risks, but because of their propensity to manage risk, these will not be risks on the scale of the full-blown entrepreneur.

They value challenge, independence, being able to demonstrate leadership and they make fast decisions.

Entrepreneur

These are people who are great to be around so long as you share their view of the world and you don't disagree with them.

They are expedient, often (though not always) socially confident, dominant, experimental, driven, decisive and thrive on risk and challenge. They will take massive personal risk, often in the defiance of any logic, tending to reframe 'failure', adapting and changing their tack to move around any obstacle.

Male entrepreneurs tend to be driven by some experience of being marginalized in their early years, such as being dyslexic or from an immigrant background. Others are driven by a sense of social injustice, often those that were born into poverty. They are driven by a burning desire never to return to their childhood experiences; this feeling of 'separation', of being different, leads to their need for autonomy and, of course, wealth creation.

Female entrepreneurs tend to be brighter overall, with 70% of them being educated to degree level. They seek autonomy and professional self development. They can achieve a level of satisfaction, which male entrepreneurs find difficult to establish. They are able to say that they have achieved what they set out to achieve, and then move on feeling fulfilled. Male entrepreneurs tend to find this very difficult indeed.

Women entrepreneurs often report being influenced by a female role model, someone that they admired. If we want to create more female entrepreneurs, it's simple: we need to expose more women to more role models.

If you are wondering if you have the mindset of the entrepreneur, you can get a good indication just by taking the *To the Edge Quick Quiz* in the appendix at the back of this book. You may even want to do the quiz before you read any further and then revisit it after you have taken in the successes, failures, high and lows of the people whose stories this book will unfold. You may find that your attitudes and beliefs have changed.

Now … to The Edge

It is possible to learn to become more enterprising, and that is what this book is about. You'll find yourself getting close to some inspirational and extraordinary people. At the end of each profile, I've included some key learning insights which are designed to help you take away what's important. These may often be small things, which if you think about them in the right way and have the courage to put them into practice, may well make a big difference.

These are insights which may well change your life.

So come on. Let's go.

Let's go and get closer to The Edge.

2

The Alchemist

'It's my favourite part of the day, and I just can't give it up. I love opening the orders. I just love it.'

The art deco Picturedrome was once a flea pit cinema which showed its last flick in 1968. Today, it has been beautifully refurbished as the headquarters and operations centre for Nimogen Ltd.

Looking down from what was the projection room, you can see that the auditorium is now an open plan office space. It houses forty workstations, all identical except for the little personal touches that each person has added. Desk number nine looks exactly like the other thirty-nine. The pictures of the occupant's wife and four daughters show he is a family man, but there are no clues to suggest that this is a space which is any more or less important than the others.

There are no symbols of the status of the individual who sits at desk number nine. At a glance you would be hard pushed to conclude that this was the team leader; you would be really stretching your imaginative powers if you thought that this was the office supervisor; in fact desk number nine belongs to the Alchemist. He is Karl Massey and he owns the business. He is as passionate about the detail of the business of selling things today as he was when he started as a teenage boy. That is enough for him not to need to surround himself with executive frippery.

He is the Alchemist. A man who performs the business equivalent of turning base metal into gold. Solid gold. He has developed a knack of buying businesses for a pound and transforming their fortunes. Today, Nimogen owns Prestons of Bolton, Wedding Ring World, The Diamond Centre of the North and Cottrills Jewellers; is the UK market leader in corporate long service and retirement awards; and will shortly launch a new business, Wedding Gift World.

It all began when a thirteen-year-old boy, who desperately wanted to please his clock maker father, agreed to spend the day helping in his small shop. It was on that day that he fell in love. He fell in love, not with the beauty or the intricacy of his father's clocks: he became besotted by the process of selling things.

Today, with a string of businesses and a turnover of £16 million, he remains head over heels in love. So much so that he still opens the orders.

Out of favour

Karl Massey can put his finger on the reason for his drive in business. Unlike many other entrepreneurs, who often have no clue as to what it is that drives them, Karl is quite clear. He says his drive came out of a desire to please his father, who continued to provide for his family amidst difficult personal circumstances, and who found it hard not to display his favouritism towards his other children over Karl. Paranoia perhaps? Wait until you hear the story.

His upbringing was not difficult in the financial sense. His father continued to run the family business, a tiny jeweller's shop in the centre of Alderley Edge. His father was the clockmaker, his grandmother worked there and there was a watchmaker. In truth, with the three of them, there wasn't a great deal of room in the tiny shop to accommodate customers.

On a beautiful summer's day in the late 1970s, a thirteen-year-old Karl Massey was lying in bed thinking about the day's skateboarding that lay ahead of him. He heard the footsteps of his father, the bedroom door swung open and his dad hit him with a surprise question.

'What are you doing today, do you want to come to work with me?'

_____

In truth, Karl knew that the answer was no. But he replied in the affirmative because more than anything he wanted to please his father. It was to be the day that was to determine the course of the rest of his life.

He recalls:

'It was a little shop with no style. It sold Beswick pottery; Timex watches; silver jewellery; second-hand jewellery and antique jewellery. He let me serve people and I loved it.'

_____

It began a love affair with the process of selling. Karl hated school and admits he was not very academic. Here he had found something that he really enjoyed and that he was good at. After that first day, he didn't need any prompting from his dad, he spent every Saturday and school holidays working in that tiny shop.

He says:

'I used to set myself a target of selling at least two Timex watches when I was there on the day.'

It must have impressed his father in some way, because a deal was done with the school that if Karl had a guaranteed job, he could leave early at the age of fifteen. So, he began working full time and found that he absolutely loved it.

Life took an exciting turn two years later, when his dad announced that he had taken on another shop in nearby Cheadle, and he was entrusting Karl to run it at the tender age of seventeen. Karl would do the buying and selling of second-hand watches and jewellery, and within five years there were four shops in the group.

Problems emerged when Karl's younger brother joined the business. Partly it was little more than the sibling rivalry you would expect from brothers, partly it was down to their difference in work ethic at the time.

'There was always a bit of animosity between us, a bit of needle, although we weren't in the same location. Partly that was my fault. I was quite aggressive, not in a physical sense, but I was always push, push, push. He was always the favourite.'

Still, the needle didn't stop Karl from dreaming dreams of what might be. In his lunch hour, he would often go just to look at other jewellers' shops. There was one store in particular that intrigued him. It was called Cottrills in Bramhall. 'It had trebled its size from a small corner shop on the front of an arcade to a big shop, all marble, very plush. I used to go and look in the windows and think, "how have they done it?"'

The answer to the sudden growth spurt was to become clear sometime later, when in the summer of 1988 it went bust. Before the growth spurt the owner had run into financial difficulties, and turned to one of his customers, Peter Clowes, for help. Clowes gave an interest free loan of £2 million in return for a 51% stake in the business. Much of the money was invested in expanding the business, but the sales didn't match the growth and Clowes sacked the owner. Shortly afterwards, the Barlow Clowes scandal came to light. Peter Clowes was sent to prison for fraudulently misappropriating £140 million worth of assets belonging to small investors in his offshore scheme. All of Barlow Clowes' assets were seized, including Cottrills.

With Cottrills in the hands of the receivers, Karl was delighted at the response of his father, which was, 'Well, let's have a go at buying it'. They had a go, and in time they struck a deal.

'The deal was that we would buy the business for a pound and buy the stock at cost price less 20%. If it hadn't worked, we had four shops to put the stock in, so we bought it. No one else really wanted it. It was a white elephant really. When we bought it, it was turning over £300,000 a year which was no good at all. I went straight in there to run it.'

Other people may have been fascinated by the extensive range of stock and the quality of the merchandise, but Karl's fascination remained for sales. He found that Cottrills had a corporate client, who about once a month would buy a gold watch for a member of staff who had done long service. It gave Karl an idea.

He put it to his dad.

'I remember my dad coming in one day. I said, "I've had an idea. I'm going to develop a corporate business, sell watches and clocks and crystal." He said "OK". I said we will have to put a brochure together and start mailing it out. He always watched the pennies. He made his own pads for the window and stuff. He said, "Well how much is it going to cost?" I replied, "I'll do the design and then we will just get it printed." So I did a very basic brochure, all the usual stuff, and started mailing it out.'

He got his first appointment with the construction company Tarmac in Wolverhampton, and he admits he didn't really know what he was doing. 'I filled this big sports bag with watches and clocks and went to see them. I didn't know what I was doing. They said OK we will use you for watches and clocks, but if they want something electrical they can go to Dixons.'

He was in business, or so he thought. Three months later he hadn't received a single order from Tarmac. He then did something which gave him a simple insight which was to enable him to see a niche for a fantastic new business. He made a phone call and listened.

'I rang them up. She said, "Well, everyone's going to Dixons." So I said, "Well, if I could put something together that included the electrical goods, and gave you 10% discount [because Dixons gave them 5%], would you use me?"'

The lady from Tarmac told him to come up with something that she could look at. He still has one of the rudimentary product portfolios that he produced for them. He went down to a local electrical retailer and explained what he was trying to do. The retailer was receptive and said that he made a 30% margin, and that they could split it three ways; a 10% discount for Tarmac; 10% for him and 10% for Karl.

Slowly but surely the orders for long service awards began to come in. Each time somebody ordered an electrical product, Karl would pick it up from the shop himself and drive it down to Wolverhampton. Next he got a piece of ICI's long service award business, and things were moving. It wasn't spectacular but he stuck at it.

One morning a large envelope arrived with a British Rail logo franked on it. As he opened it he remembered that they had been one of the firms he had mailed out to. Inside the envelope was a tender document. They had a long service scheme and wanted someone who could provide a range of around sixty products covering the usual watches, clocks and electrical goods, and extending it to include garden furniture and DIY equipment.

Karl roped in his Saturday boy, Martin, to help with the tender. They sourced suppliers for the products in the range and where they couldn't, made a few guesses about what price they could supply them for. Together they worked with their printer to produce a mock-up brochure which British Rail would be able to give out to staff qualifying for long service awards, and they sent it in with their tender. They were shortlisted and a date was arranged for two buyers and a representative from Human Resources to come and visit Karl.

To visit what? A jeweller's shop? Hardly something that would impress a company wanting access to a diverse range of some sixty different products. Karl was undeterred. He simply emptied his jeweller's shop, and he and Martin set about transforming it into a long service awards showroom – for the day of the visit at least.

He remembers:

'It was good fun. Some of the products were a problem. They wanted a collapsible ladder that you could make into different shapes. We couldn't find one. Anyway, we eventually found one in Argos. For the actual presentation to British Rail, Martin went to Argos and bought some of the items we couldn't source. Argos were pitching for the business as well which was quite funny. We set them up as though they were ours and BR came and looked at them. Then we packed them up and took them back to Argos for a refund.'

The delegation from British Rail was impressed. They told Karl he had made it to the final two in the tender competition and a little later he got a phone call.

'They said, "You have got it, but we need to see your audited accounts". I didn't have any because the business had just been trading as a separate entity for just over twelve months. So I went to see them and I was prepared to say that I didn't have any, but in the end they didn't ask so I got away with it.'

It was a good thing he got away with it, because this contract was to transform his fledgling business.
He says:

'The estimated contract value was a million pounds, but because of privatization they spent nearly £1 million with us in the first six months and £1.5 million with us in the first year. They got rid of loads of people. If they had done a minimum of ten years or were at retirement age they could choose a gift from our brochure.'

The break-up of the rail network represented the build up of Karl's new business in quite a dramatic way. In 1993, turnover grew from £300,000 to £2.5 million. The BR business helped tremendously, but Karl was able to keep adding new corporate clients because his competitors didn't notice the need to change.

'People like Garrard, the Crown Jewellers, Mappin & Webb who had the Royal Warrant, and little jewellers all over the country were into this corporate business. They sold themselves primarily as jewellers, so they wouldn't move into associated products. As a result, we were winning loads and loads of business. So that was the turning point at which we became a serious and profitable business. I thought differently, I didn't think as a jeweller, I just saw an opportunity to sell merchandise.'

In addition, he has a natural hunger. His first thought on winning the BR business was that if they lost it they would be back to square one, so he redoubled his efforts to expand the customer base.

His passion for selling merchandise is quite clear. When asked what were the top three long service gifts chosen in 1993, he doesn't hesitate for even a moment:

'The single most popular gift was the VCA-30HM video recorder. We did 3000 in the year; the CD-150E was the hi-fi system; and the CV-3730 was the portable telly. Those were the top three. All electrical.'

BR extended the contract for another year and did £3 million worth of business in just those first two years. Karl still holds contracts with most of the independent rail operating companies today.

Of course, the days when he went to the electrical retailers and put the goods in the back of his car had to stop, and he struck a deal with Sharp Electronics to supply his electrical goods at a much higher margin. Within a short time he was one of their top ten independent account holders, spending more than £1 million a year with them.

This corporate business was now becoming serious and Karl and his father put it into a separate company called Nimogen, named after Karl's daughters Natasha and Imogen. They split the shares 50:50.

Out of the blue, Karl's father was to drop a bombshell. He remembers:

'As the business grew we started talking about the subject of inheritance. What would happen with the shares when something happened to him or my mother? So we reached an agreement. My brother would inherit the family business which was the jewellers' shops, my sister would inherit his private assets and house, and his shares in the business would revert to me, which I was happy with.

'The business needed a bigger firm of accountants and at the first meeting the new accountants began to work through a checklist of issues. When they got to the issue of inheritance and succession, I outlined my understanding of what was to happen. My father interrupted saying, "Well that *was* the case, but you've crossed me a few times over the years, so my shareholding isn't coming to you any more." I said, "Where's it going?" He said "Well, it will be to your brother and sister or their children or both." So he had effectively cut me out of the will, and broke the news to me in front of three accountants and my Financial Director at the time.'

Karl remembers it as a time when it seemed a bit like World War III had just broken out, but his father refused to back down. He did eventually agree that he would sell his shareholding in Nimogen to Karl, who agreed to buy the shares over twenty-five years. They have never spoken since the day the deal was signed.

It was a journey which had its origins in a desire to please his father. Despite Karl's extraordinary business success, it seems that it is the one thing he will never be able to do.

He was out of favour and out of pocket, and it couldn't have come at a worse time.

Bombshells come in threes

The buyout of the shares in Nimogen wasn't cheap. It was a low overhead company with a very healthy turnover, massive growth and great profit margins. Nimogen also owned the Cottrills jewellers shop in Bramhall that had been bought for a pound and another in Macclesfield. So Karl's father's shares represented a major financial commitment.

Still, the corporate business just seemed too good to be true. It had grown at an average of 30% a year for thirteen years. Suddenly, after his father's bombshell, orders started to slow down. Business began to drop off for the first time ever. Now it was falling by 25–30% every month.

Karl couldn't understand it. Was this some kind of a curse? A jinx?

This was the worst possible news, because before his father's bombshell he had committed to opening another Cottrills store in Wilmslow. These are expensive to set up. In addition to fit-out costs, staff and marketing, a store like that would need at least £1.5 million worth of stock just to appear credible. He was so far down the line with this there was no way out. Bombshells come in threes.

How do you deal with three bombshells? One at a time it would seem. In relation to his father's shares in Nimogen, he swallowed hard and agreed the price. The downturn in corporate business was another matter. He just couldn't understand it. Why after thirteen successive years of spectacular growth had it just suddenly slumped?

Then, in a flash, it came to him. He says:

> 'The two big periods that companies recognize for long service awards are 15 years' and 25 years' service. If you rewind 25 years from 2005 to 1980 and 15 years to 1990, both were the start of big recessionary periods. We only deal with major corporations and their recruitment slows down in these periods. They were laying people off, not taking them on, all these years ago.'

These recessionary periods were hitting Karl's business like aftershocks in an earthquake. The unfortunate thing was that two were hitting him at the same time. Yet he believed that if he could weather the storm the business would upturn again

18

to mirror the growing economies of the mid to late 1980s and 1990s. He was right. In 2007 the business is going in the right direction again and he now has more than 550 corporate clients.

Then there was the little matter of how to create a flagship Cottrills store in Wilmslow. You would think under this kind of pressure he might tone down his ambitions a little. But no. Karl continued to expand his thinking. He remembers going into the empty building:

'The actual building was an Electricity Board building, art deco, 1930s. Pete, who does my shop-fitting work, and I went into this huge empty space with loads of pillars. So I stood right in the centre and said, "Why don't we do a floor to ceiling marine aquarium, and then around it we will do a champagne bar in the form of a breaking wave and clad it in bronze." It just came to me! So he clads the pillars in marble then he had the idea of cladding the walls with birds-eye maple, so that the grain in the panels matches up and flows right around the room. We tend to go for a pint after work and say what about this, what about that, and it just sort of happens.'

Out of these outlandish ideas and a few pints after work, something quite spectacular happened. The Wilmslow branch of Cottrills was awarded Best New Jewellery Shop of the Year in the Jewellery Awards, and then *Retail Week* voted it one of the 100 most inspirational stores in the world next to the Louis Vuitton store in Paris. It is a spectacular setting, and the backdrop to what Karl refers to as an 'experience', made all the more pleasant by the constant supply of free champagne. He says:

'We try to make it a really, really pleasant experience. You've got to differentiate yourself. You can buy a Rolex from a number of jewellers, multiples or independents, it's a brand and in some ways a commodity. We want customers to come to us and relish the experience and enjoy the environment.'

People do. As well as all the top brand watches and diamond engagement rings, customers can buy a mobile phone. That is as long as it is one of the Vertu Constellation range starting at £2500 and going up to about £21,000 for the gold model. Cottrills sells about forty of these every year, whilst diamond rings go up to the £60,000 mark, and last year's biggest single sale was a £120,000 Rolex watch.

The bombshells, it seems, have been well and truly deflected. But why stop there?

A pound for Preston's

Just a year after taking on the Wilmslow site for Cottrills, a famous name in the jewellery business went bust. In the 1970s Preston's of Bolton was one of the most famous jewellery stores in England. The old visitors books show that people would travel to 'The Diamond Centre of the North' from as far as Cornwall and Scotland to get their engagement rings there. On one single day in the 1970s it sold 168 wedding rings.

With all his other issues ongoing, it wasn't the best time to be taking on something new, but Karl's enthusiasm got the better of him.

'The timing was absolutely dreadful, but I just knew it was a fantastic opportunity, so I bought it. They had about seven stores but I just wanted the Bolton one because in the seventies and eighties it was the most famous jewellery store in the country. Everybody knew it. They all went there for their engagement and wedding rings.'

The shop was a large corner unit in Bolton, but it was quite run-down. Karl splashed out.

'I bought the business for a pound and I got Preston's of Bolton, Diamond Centre of the North and Wedding Ring World for the same pound.'

There was a slight catch. He also had to buy stock, but in audacious stroke of entrepreneurial genius, he did. He bought £2.3 million worth of stock for £1.5 million, which he was able to sell in just four months as a closing down sale, then he closed the shop and refurbished it. He closed down the Bramhall and Macclesfield branches to fund this and the new Wilmslow store.

Rather than lose all the Bramhall and Macclesfield business, Karl took action to redirect it to Wilmslow, using direct mail and promoting the Wilmslow store as a destination experience. Today the Wilmslow store turns over almost the same as Bramhall, Macclesfield and Wilmslow combined did in 2005, on just one third of the cost base. In addition he acquired the three brand names from Preston's of Bolton, and refurbished a fantastic store in Bolton at a net cost of very little indeed.

As a result, with just two stores pre-2005, his retail turnover was £3.5 million and today with two different stores his turnover is £7 million.

The Alchemist had turned base metal to gold again, yet he remains refreshingly modest about it all. He says:

'It sounds quite straightforward and in a way it was. It's not a complicated business. Business is about finding new and interesting ways of selling things and adding value, because everybody was trying to flog watches.'

Others might base themselves at the glamorous end of the business, in one of the world's most striking stores, basking in the glory and sipping the occasional glass of champagne. Not Karl Massey, he seems happiest at desk number nine in the Picturedrome nerve centre of his operation, working on the next developments for the business, looking at how he can tie himself tighter to his existing clients, trying to get into their shoes and see things from their perspective. He says, 'I found out quite quickly that a long service award is a nuisance purchase for any HR department. When I go and see a client now I don't say this is the brochure and these are the products, I sell them the full service so all they have to do every month is email my admin team an Excel spreadsheet with the name and address of every qualifier. On behalf of the client we send out the long service pack to the recipient, using their letterhead and agreed text. We even have their Chairman's signature on it.

'Our message is, "give it us and we will do it all for you". We make our profit by selling them the merchandise and adding value. They don't want to do it; they want to be doing their normal HR stuff. It ties us tighter to the customer.'

This year, they will double the number of products in their awards range and are establishing a new web based service called Wedding Gift World, which essentially sells the same range of merchandise to a different target market – wedding guests. To develop the corporate market more, gifts are now being promoted as incentives and Karl has launched the Aspirations voucher, which companies can buy in denominations from £5–£500 and give to their staff as incentives and rewards. Staff may then redeem their rewards by choosing a gift from the range.

Karl is optimistic about the future, and why shouldn't he be? He says:

'I love the business. I love the corporate and the retail. We've had two tricky years, every business has them, but we have come through it now and it's a nice feeling.

'There's always something that gives you a nice buzz. My favourite part of the day, and I can't give it up, is opening the orders. Because most of them come in by Freepost, some are internet, phone and fax but 80% still come in by post. I love opening the orders. I just love it, because you are seeing what people are choosing. That's the most enjoyable bit.'

Meanwhile, the team in the Picturedrome are all busy working away, dealing with up to 800 orders a week, whilst the warehouse is busy shipping out up to 4000 items a week. In the Bolton shop, diamonds are flying through the door, and in Wilmslow the champagne continues to flow.

Yet nobody here is resting on their laurels, least of all the occupant of desk number nine. He is the man who will be unable to resist opening the orders in the morning. He is the man who is turning business base metal into gold.

He is the Alchemist.

Entrepreneurial insights from the Alchemist

- Look for and act on those small insights. People often overcomplicate things and believe that for a business to be good it has to be highly complicated, technical and founded on in-depth analysis. So often, as Karl Massey has shown, it is simply about noticing and acting upon small insights. When he hadn't received a single order from Tarmac after three months he did a simple thing – he asked why. He could have just given up on it there and then, but he acted on the insight and became a supplier of electrical goods as well as jewellery. When he realized that arranging and ordering long service awards was one of the jobs Human Resources departments hated, he acted on this insight as well, by supplying the full administration service as well as the gifts. He has taken away a nuisance job from them and brought his company even closer to the client.

- Iconic design acts as a magnet. Karl is fortunate in that he has on board a talented shop-fitter in the form of Peter Dooley. This means that, over a few pints of beer, they were able to envision something that became one of the world's most inspirational stores. I have noticed in other work I am involved in, particularly as an adviser to sporting organizations, how iconic design can have a transformational effect. For Karl's business it has increased its visibility, added value to the customer experience and enabled him to channel customers from locations where he has closed down shops, so that he now has double the turnover with one third of the cost base. Elaborate design plans may seem expensive, but if you really know what you are doing and why you are doing it, you can achieve a great return. Go and have a couple of pints and think about it.

- Differentiation is the key. Karl is continually looking for new ways to differentiate his business from his competitors. That's how he got into the corporate side of the business in the first place. Find ways to differentiate your product, whatever it is, and you will delight your customers, fight off competitors and tie yourself tighter to your clients.

- Maximize your chance opportunities. Without even thinking about it, Karl practises all four elements in the science of luck – maximize your chance opportunities; listen to your intuition; believe in good fortune; and turn bad luck to good. Professor Richard Wiseman has shown through a series of experiments that people who enjoy more than their fair share of good fortune do these four things consistently. For more on the science of luck, see my book *Bear Hunt – Earn your living by doing what you love*, Chapter Five.

3

The Soapstar

'It's 3am and I'm in bed randomly calling out names for a new
restaurant concept.'

The scene. A book launch for *Your Own Worst Enemy*, a fictionalized account
of the diaries of Vietnam veteran Barney Adams. Fiona Thompson, the author,
addresses a small gathering and receives polite applause. Outside the bookshop,
the mood is less friendly. She is hassled by a nosy reporter and three hostile men,
concerned that eventually the true names of the people in Barney's diary will come
to light.

As the mood becomes ugly a minor scuffle ensues between one of the men,
Harry, and Andy, Fiona's friend. A stranger appears, jacket draped over his shoul-
der, it is Chris Bainbridge …

Chris: (To Harry's mate) Hey. Listen mate. I think you had better take
your friend home.

Harry: (To Fiona) And who's this? A friend of yours, eh?

Chris: Listen. You better just clear off. Nobody wants any trouble.

Harry: (growls at Fiona before being led off by his two mates) You
haven't heard the last of this.

Fiona: (Turning to Chris) Thank you. That was just so embarrassing.

Chris: Hey, don't worry about it. I'm Chris Adams, Barney's nephew.

Fiona: I didn't know Barney had a nephew.

In actual fact he didn't. Chris Adams was really a pseudonym for Chris Bainbridge, and before the episode was out he would deliver Fiona a parcel containing a carpet snake and purport to rescue her from it.

All in a day's work for a soap star. For Tim Bacon, soap star turned entrepreneur, this scene was his first day's work as Chris Bainbridge, on the Australian soap *Sons & Daughters*.

When he came over to England to make it big as an actor, he took a job in a restaurant. This started a love affair so captivating that he forgot all about acting, and today he is the boss of Living Ventures, a 34-strong chain of restaurants which he has built in just eight years.

A trombone-playing, Tasmanian thespian cocktail waiter, who creates one successful business after another whilst in a seemingly dreamlike state, really does sound like a storyline from a soap opera, but as you are about to find out, this is the incredible story of the rise and rise of Tim Bacon.

As for Tim's alter ego *Chris Bainbridge*, he went on for another 138 episodes, living what might now be considered a fairly sedate life in the Australian soap-suburbs; sending Fiona a dead spider and dumping manure on her drive, before stalking her through the woods at Woombai, threatening to kill her, and being run down by a jeep. After he had treatment in a psychiatric hospital, he began a relationship with Fiona which went sour when she took in an illegal Vietnamese immigrant, Nguyen Hung. Chris saved Hung's life after he was bitten by a deadly funnel spider, and just as he was becoming more tolerant of him, Chris's father, also released from a psychiatric institution, pulls a gun on Fiona, but then turns it on himself. In episode 688, Chris bids a tearful farewell.

Chris Bainbridge packed a lot into his 139 episodes, and in-between, Tim Bacon had become a star.

The view from Tazzie

Statistically speaking, you are as likely to meet someone from Equatorial Guinea or Transnistria as you are a Tasmanian. They make up just 0.008% of the world's population. Officially, of course, they are Australians, though many Tasmanians wonder if Australians share that view. It is not uncommon for Tasmania, a small island about 240 km off the coast of Victoria, to be inadvertently left off maps printed in official documents.

Tim Bacon is a Tasmanian with a mixed provenance. His father grew up in the East End of London, and emigrated to Australia after working the 'apple run' ships between Liverpool and Sydney. His mother was a Dutch émigré and Tim was born in England during a brief return to the UK before they returned to settle in Tasmania.

So his memories of growing up are all Tasmanian. When you look at the research that suggests that entrepreneurs are trying to escape some feeling of 'separation', a feeling of being different, it's easy to imagine that maybe you have uncovered the secrets of Tim's success.

He has been after all, part of a minority group on the edge of the world; a Tasmanian in Australia; an Australian in the UK; and an actor in the world of business. Lots of reasons to feel different, yet Tim Bacon doesn't describe it that way:

> 'I didn't feel separate. I have always been aware of my own individuality. I've always felt individual.'

He remembers Tasmania with great affection. He loved music, played the trombone, played a lot of sport and did drama. Those are his memories, and it was drama in which he showed his first glimmer of entrepreneurial spirit.

> 'I was part of a group of ten people who set up a drama group. We would give drama lessons and put on shows with kids, and we charged for it.'

Idyllic as it was, it was difficult for Tim not to want to look across the horizon and imagine what lay beyond. He says:

> 'The view of the world from Tasmania is unusual. The world just looks like a very big place, very exciting with lots of things to do.'

When he wanted to pursue one of his great loves and go to drama school in Tasmania, he fell foul of his stepfather who put the brakes on his ambitions. He decided it was time to see what lay beyond the horizon. He left home, and, at the age of nineteen, landed in Sydney and enrolled at drama school.

He never did finish the course. About halfway through he went out and got himself an agent, and before he knew it he got a call to go to an audition for *Sons & Daughters*. He showed the level of his self belief:

> 'The part was to last six weeks, but I packed in the drama course anyway. The job lasted a year and a half, and I did some film and theatre work as well. I was one of the few actors actually making money out of it.'

At the time the Aussie soap was the big thing on TV. It was the highest-rated programme in its slot, and the most watched Aussie soap of the 1980s. Tim found himself a reluctant star. He remembers:

> 'I was getting chased through parks and out of supermarkets. I wasn't keen on being recognized. I like being recognized for my work. Look at all these awards.' He gestures towards the awards that cover the shelves in his boardroom. They are not Emmys or Oscars. They are all from the restaurant and catering industry. 'I just didn't like the soap star lifestyle. I was never going to win an Oscar for acting but we have won the catering industry's equivalent.'

Thank God it's Friday

In 1979, Tim headed for the UK, to see if he could make it as an actor. Most actors take jobs as waiters or bartenders at some time when they are between jobs. They tend to speak about these jobs with disdain or embarrassment. Not Tim Bacon. He positively fizzes with excitement when he recalls his first job in the UK.

> 'I got a job at TGI Friday's. I just loved it. It was like a performance. It was a totally groundbreaking idea at the time. You got six weeks training in how to make cocktails, and then you were allowed to project your own personality – something I've always tried to take on board in my own businesses.'

He got great at making cocktails. So much so that he won a competition to find the best cocktail waiter in London and found himself making cocktails on *The Terry Wogan Show*. It was a turning point. He says:

> 'I won this bartending competition and went on *Terry Wogan*. I was supposed to be on for just a couple of minutes and I ended up staying for the whole of the latter half of the show serving drinks to the guests. The next day the phone went crazy. I had ten customers in the first day wanting me to show their staff how to do this.'

He realized that there was money to be made, and he set up a consultancy business to go into new start-up restaurants and deliver the kind of ethos he had experienced at TGI Friday's. It mushroomed. At one time he had fourteen trainers, expert in every aspect of the business. With more than seventy clients under his belt, the business was good to him, yet he wasn't completely happy. A couple of things were bothering him. Firstly, the consultancy projects were short-term hits, and he wasn't always convinced that the kind of concept that they were trying to deliver could be properly bedded down in the three-month period that was typical of their assignments. Secondly, although he had a good business, there were no tangible assets. He says:

'It was a lifestyle business and I wanted something that I could really grow.'

So he let the consultancy business run down and took some time out to think and look around, and to work out what he wanted to do next. He describes it as a piece of luck, but entrepreneurs tend to make their own luck.

By now it was 1993 and a bar in Manchester's Deansgate, JW Johnson's, had just gone into receivership, so Tim and a friend bought it with a view to turning it around. It was tougher than they had imagined. Tim says:

'It was the first time I had managed. Consultancy is about advising and you can walk away after three months. I realized that you have to have tremendous endurance to be able to manage well. I like to get systems in place so I know that I can sit with a drink and a paper and know everything is running as it should. After three months of hard work that's how it was.'

A kind of formula was being unfolded. One that had sharp systems yet was run by real people with personalities who could create an ambience. Tim and business partner Jeremy Roberts then created the Via Vita restaurant concept and sold when the chain had four restaurants. It wasn't always easy though. Tim remembers the first one.

'It was in Birmingham and it absolutely bombed. We thought it would take off over Christmas. On New Year's Eve we had about ten people. We had doubled the turnover from £5000 to £10,000 a week, but with our overheads that was no good. We sat down on New Year's Day and thought, "What are we going to do?"'

They decided that they had to get hands-on. The General Manager was re-moved and Tim drove to Birmingham every day. After three months it was turning over £20,000 to £30,000 a week and they were back in business.

They then went on to develop the Life Café concept in Liverpool and Manchester, selling this to Whitbread in 1999 and retaining the management contract.

In the Living Room

Now they were in a position to do something of scale, and they formed a team around them drawn from their past operations. All the team were given shares in the new company, Living Ventures.

Their first concept was the Living Room, an up-tempo casual dining restaurant and piano bar, set in a contemporary style setting with a colonial twist. Ironically, the very first Living Room was, and still is, in the old JW Johnson's building, Tim's original operation.

It soon became known as 'the staff canteen' for Premiership footballers and the brand has become strong as new sites have appeared in another twelve locations from Edinburgh to London – which has its own mutation, Living Room W1. The beauty of the Living Room concept is that it has optional modules so the thirteen sites are not identical. Living Rooms can be mixed and matched with a number of different modules. The add-ons include the high-energy lounge-style Mosquito bar, the more traditional Dining Room restaurant, and the non-fee-paying private members bars, The Study and The Vampire Suite.

Mosquito is a high-energy cocktail bar, nightclub and live music venue which has a huge bed that transforms into the centre stage – literally, it opens out to form the stage for live acts.

Then in 2005, the Living Room group bought nineteen restaurants in the Est, Est, Est chain for £16.4 million, and spent £500,000 on a new look. They took on a development chef from Italy and invested in staff training. The first revamped Est, Est, Est was in Alderley Edge. In its first week of operation under Living Ventures new regime, its like-for-like sales were up 174%.

This sort of impressive ability to turn things around and ramp up the performance of his restaurants has been a hallmark of Tim Bacon's career. Living Ventures now turns over something in the region of £50 million per year and in December 2005, the group was named the 34th fastest-growing company in the UK in the Sunday Times top 100, thanks to an annual sales growth of 99.25% between 2001 and 2004.

So how come he has such a Midas touch? Perhaps it is down to the philosophy. Tim says:

'We believe that everyone has to get a fair deal. The customers, the staff and the business. Unlike most other restaurants, our staff get to keep their tips. If they make £200 a night in tips, why should they have to share it with people who may not be performing as well as they are? We try to create an ambience so that the customers feel like they own part of the place.'

He has always been aware of his own individuality, and he likes to put his stamp on a place. He says:

'I love thinking about concepts. Wherever I go I'm thinking about new concepts. It drives my wife Karine mad. The good thing is that she has started to do it now.'

It is true, all the Living Ventures concepts have quite a distinctive stamp, and Tim wouldn't dream of leaving it to some marketing agency to brand them. He likes to come up with the names for the new restaurant concepts himself. He remembers, vaguely at least, how he came up with his first one.

'I was on a boozy night out with a DJ in Liverpool and I was going through all sorts of names. All I remember is that when I woke up in the morning, The Living Room just stuck with me.'

On a trip to Belfast, he was intrigued by a bar called Fly.

'I thought, "I like that idea". The idea of a bug being the name of a bar. So I started to go through other bugs. Cockroach, dragonfly, hornet – and then I hit on mosquito. I liked the sound of it. I could see it.'

It is a good name for a cocktail bar, in fact it could almost be the name of a cocktail.
Then there was Blackhouse Grills.

'It's 3 a.m. and I'm in bed randomly calling out names for a new restaurant concept. My wife Karine just wanted to go to sleep. When I got to the name Blackhouse, she just said, "That's it. Now go to sleep." I slept on it and when I tried it out in the morning, I liked it.'

31

With the Blackhouse Grills, the Soapstar has created a very special steak and seafood experience. Not just your run of the mill 'surf and turf' fare here, the pride of place on the menu goes to the eight-ounce Kobe steak at £50 a head. The Japanese Wagyu cattle are massaged in beer four times a day and played classical music. It gives a unique tenderness and taste that would make you ... well, pay fifty pounds for it.

It's clear that he loves the imaginative, creative side of the business. He says:

> 'I love thinking about the concepts so much. Often I will go into this semi-dreamlike state. There's nothing better when you are sitting in a chair and the sun is coming through the conservatory and there you are in this dreamlike state just thinking about new concepts. I'm not really interested in anything else.'

He doesn't even seem to have a great deal of interest in the competition. It's almost as if it is a case of 'don't worry about the competition; let them worry about you'. This is not arrogance or a flippant disregard for competition; Tim seems to adopt the attitude that, if you concentrate on what is important, the rest will look after itself.

Alderley Edge itself is a good case in point. The flagship Est, Est, Est, restaurant has done very well in the face of stiff competition from the long-established Alderley Bar & Grill. Now, in a street not even 500 yards long, there is more competition brewing as Heathcote's London Road has opened, following hot on the heels of La Vina, and adding to The Bubble Room, two Chinese, an Indian and a Turkish restaurant, with all sorts of rumours circulating about future openings by other competitors.

Tim's approach is to continue to set high standards and expectations for his managers and to get them to constantly raise their game, which in his view means raising it for the customer, the staff and in turn for the business. He still spends two days a week going out to the shop floor, gauging the feel of his restaurants and looking at performance. As he says, 'The performance figures don't lie.'

Right now, the Est, Est, Est chain needs some work. Inevitably it will take time to get the whole portfolio to peak performance. The effort to make this happen means that Living Ventures is in a period where it has to 'stick to the knitting' for a while. Tim says:

> 'It's a bit like an airport holding pattern: we are bringing each Est restaurant in, one at a time.'

When I ask about his approach to underperforming General Managers, it is revealing. 'Perhaps' I proffer helpfully, 'you suggest that they develop a turnaround plan rather rapidly.' He laughs at this, and smiles at the thought. 'Yes. Yes. "Suggest". I like that word. "Suggest" is a nice way of putting it.' He laughs again at this. It is clear that this is a man who is in the business of making incisive, difficult decisions and will make them. That's just his business. It is not personal.

There will be more difficult decisions for Tim before the 'holding pattern' phase of Living Ventures is finally concluded, and you sense that he longs for that moment. It will be a moment when he can start to do what he likes to do best. To pluck new ideas and concepts out of his semi-dreamlike states whilst he relaxes in his conservatory.

There is definitely more to come from this trombone-playing, Tasmanian thespian. In the meantime he kindly offers to let me have the Est, Est, Est restaurant in Alderley Edge for the launch of this book.

If his first episode of *Sons and Daughters* is anything to go by, Tim Bacon aka Chris Bainbridge might be a useful fellow to have around at a book launch.

Entrepreneurial insights from the Soapstar

- Allow yourself to get into the imaginative zone. Research shows that great ideas, great concepts, are less likely to come when we are stressed and in formal environments. When we are relaxed, chemicals which affect the creative side of the brain are triggered. Tim refers to this as his semi-dreamlike state. A state which has produced great ideas from The Living Room, to Mosquito, to Blackhouse Grills. To produce really great ideas, an appreciation of the value of allowing an imaginative phase is essential. Often businesses scoff at this idea and want to get down to 'brass tacks'. No wonder they run out of ideas. For more on the imaginative phase and how to bring more creative thinking into your business and your life, see my other book, *Bear Hunt – Earn your living by doing what you love,* Chapter 7, *Think Like an Eight Year Old.*

- See your customers as 'stakeholders' in your business, not as 'punters'. Tim feels that business really works when everyone is getting a fair deal – customers, staff and the business. He feels that customers should have the feeling that the restaurant partly belongs to them.

- You don't always need a branding agency to package your business concept; it can be an absolute delight to do it yourself. Tim loves developing the concept and dreaming up the names of his restaurants most of all.

With a turnover nearing £50 million, perhaps there is something in it. Get wrapped up in your own concept and give it your stamp.

● Get hands-on. Though eventually you want to be working on the business rather than in it, nothing beats understanding the detail of your business model and how it works. Understand the key variables and if something goes wrong, you can quickly diagnose what you can do about it. However big you get, stay close to the shop floor. Tim spends two days a week out there, checking the ambience and performance of his business from the front line.

4

The Rover

'Money can tear a person apart and make them into a horrible creature.
It can also bring out the best and make them an unbelievable person.'

The Rover's workspace is quite unusual. It is exactly 16.5 metres by 40.3 metres. Just to remind him where his domain begins and ends, white lines are drawn onto the green surface.

A white circle is placed in a central area of the workspace. It will be used should he or any of his colleagues commit a misdemeanour, and he is very protective of one particular space. It comprises two vertical pieces of wood 2.44 metres high. They are supporting another long horizontal piece of wood, and behind these is lashed the kind of net that one would expect to encounter in a picturesque Turkish fishing village.

Unusually, his colleagues spend most of their time with their backs turned towards him. Not that he is unpopular. He has a special skill, and they rely on him to make crucial decisions and interventions. In a world where we have become accustomed to flexible and virtual working, his presence in his workspace is essential. He cannot hot-desk or log in from home. He has to be there, and in a quaint throwback to the nineteenth century roots of his profession, a long whistle blows to denote the start of his shift. He continues working until he hears two short toots of the whistle followed by a final prolonged one. Then he may go home.

He is happy when he goes home with a clean sheet. In a business which talks telephone numbers, if he achieves a zero he is considered a hero.

He is of course a goalkeeper. He is at the peak of his profession and his name is Brad Friedel, the Rover. Currently the last line of defence for one-time Premier League Champions, Blackburn Rovers.

In a good and prolonged career, an average Premiership footballer will earn £25 million in wages alone. Enough money never to have to work again.

Yet Brad Friedel will continue to work. He has found within himself an enterprising nature and a genuine desire to help other people. He is showing that succeeding in business and making a social contribution are not mutually exclusive. In fact they are symbiotic.

His soccer academy in his home State of Ohio, USA, helped him to get planning permission for retail and commercial developments on a portion of the site. Part of the profits from the development in turn feed into the soccer academy helping to make it a self-sustaining, not-for-profit outfit, which is as much about helping people to find their way in life as it is about finding the stars of the future.

Bling free zone

Shortly after meeting Brad Friedel, you begin to realize how powerful media images can be in shaping our perceptions of our world. Due to little more than a handful of high-profile people, many of us carry a negative perception of today's breed of professional footballers. They have an image of being self-centred, bling encrusted brats with their brains in their feet. By contrast, Brad is calm, courteous and humble.

Whilst some players find it hard to cope when they hit the big time, Brad Friedel has more than coped. He has created a business and a future out of what started as a hobby, and has combined it with his academy project which will give kids from all sorts of backgrounds the opportunity to sample some of the experiences that have helped to shape him and who he is.

It is clear that he has little more than a passing interest in material things. 'For example,' he says, 'do you see my watch?' He holds out both arms. I am thrown for a moment as I stare at his two bare wrists. 'What kind of a trick question is this?' I think. 'I don't have one', he says, and I am relieved that, had I responded to the question, I would have got the answer right. He simply has no desire to take part in the circus that is competing to see who has the biggest, brashest, most expensive wristwatch.

He reflects on his position and says:

'I think because my dad ran into some financial problems when I was growing up, that maybe subconsciously I've given a bit more respect to the dollar. I've never been a follower of fashion. I don't need the flash watch, just little things. My phone is whatever is the free one you get with the twelve-month contract.'

He still maintains the demeanour of a nice boy from the small town of Bay Village, Ohio, the place where he grew up, and you get the feeling that even with wealth beyond his wildest dreams, he could go home tomorrow and blend in as if nothing had happened. But a lot has happened to this small-town boy who grew up with a natural aptitude for sports.

At first, things happened because of his natural athleticism. He remembers:

> 'I played all the other sports. I got offered a basketball scholarship at college. My favourite sport growing up as a youngster was ice hockey. I played that a tremendous amount of my time. The only problem with that is that I would have had to leave home at a young age, and I didn't love hockey enough to want to do that at the time – when I was 13–14.'

For a boy who was reluctant to leave home, it is interesting that his football career took him all over the world. He became 'a rover', moving around until he was able to qualify for a work permit enabling him to play in the Premier League – the best league in the world.

Then, he started to make things happen as part of a journey that was intellectual as well as physical. The Rover arrived at the Rovers in rather a roundabout way. He came via California, Nottingham, Newcastle, Sunderland, Denmark, Turkey, Columbus and, finally, Liverpool.

It was a journey that helped a small-town boy to get a great education, learn about the world and establish a reputation as an Olympian and an elite athlete. It was a journey that allowed him to dabble with opportunity and discover an enterprising mind, which switches on as his technical skill switches off for the day.

This is an uncommon combination. Research suggests that people are either technical/professional or enterprising in nature – but rarely both. Perhaps it is the precisely defined nature of his technical/professional existence that allows his mind to make the switch-over. He can walk out of one arena and into another.

In his day job as a goalkeeper, there are clearly defined rules. His workspace, the penalty area, is laid out with precision, and he is held immediately and publicly accountable for misdemeanours, mistakes and misjudgements. He has to apply an intuitive understanding of geometry and the laws of physics to make instantaneous risk assessments about the action he should take in relation to the flight of a spherical object. Then, in an instant, he will find out if his assessment of his physical capability was correct. If he gets all these calculations right he will make a save. If he can save he will prosper. Save and prosper seems to be the philosophy that Brad takes with him into the enterprising side of his life.

When the whistle blows he seems to be able to make a remarkable transformation in the way he thinks. He walks out of an arena which is highly defined, regimented, rule based and where uncertainty is dealt with through instantaneous risk assessment and intervention. The results of his actions are known there and then. There are no grey areas. He knows at the end of each working shift if he has had a good day 'at the office'.

When he walks into his enterprising arena, he is faced with a different set of variables. There are no rules about how to make a winning play in business. The variables are sometimes visible, sometimes unexpected and often have a high degree of unpredictability. The results may not become clear for weeks, months, even years. The landscape is awash with grey areas.

Perhaps it is because Brad came into business slowly at first, almost as a hobby, that has enabled him to get comfortable with making this shift in his thinking. He gave himself time to adapt, he began to understand the variables and he began to get comfortable assessing a new set of angles and risks. He also did what goalkeepers do naturally. He made a decision, after relying on someone else, to take personal responsibility.

Win, win, win

Just like many other enterprising people, Brad attributes many of the turning points in his life to luck, or serendipity. Yet luck is really about spotting opportunity, making judgements and taking action – the stock-in-trade of a goalkeeper.

His journey really started when he got himself selected for the US Youth National Team and he got noticed. He says:

> 'I was lucky in a sense that the coach was there at the right time and took me out when I was seventeen, to UCLA. It is one of the bigger universities and it had a lot of good players.'

———————————

So it was a case of 'California, here I come'. For Brad it was a great opportunity to play soccer with the top players of the time, and it introduced him to something that would later form the basis of his business ideas. He studied history and urban planning and really got switched on by the lectures on architecture. In 1992 he became part of the US Olympic soccer team that went to Barcelona and rubbed shoulders with the 'Dream Team' US basketball heroes including Magic Johnson, Michael Jordan and Larry Bird.

He didn't strike gold, or silver or bronze, but, again, he got noticed.

> 'I just got lucky and Ronnie Fenton, who was Brian Clough's [the man-

ager of Nottingham Forest] Chief Executive at the time, saw me and invited me over for a trial.'

Clough was impressed, and wanted Brad to sign for Forest right away. It was a chance to play in the Premiership, but it wasn't to be. There were tight restrictions on UK work permits which meant that only seasoned international players could qualify. At this time Brad was still a beginner.

It would be five years and thousands of miles on the clock before he would crack the work permit problem. In the meantime, the Olympic experience had given Brad some money that he thought he should invest, and it was this experience that led to him taking his destiny into his own hands.

He recalls:

'I've had investments where I've lost. It's impossible to go through life only winning. I think of it as a learning curve. I was a young kid with a financial adviser. He'd say do this, do that, I'd say OK, OK. Then you lose a little bit and you think, "I should have looked into that". It's all a learning curve.

'I learned that I knew absolutely nothing about mutual funds when I got into it. I learned that I knew absolutely nothing about the stock market when I was twenty-one years old and I vowed never to go back into it again until I knew something about it. When you look back there are certain investments that lose money. The financial adviser didn't lose money. He got his money. So who's the clever one in that deal?'

The goalkeeper was about to start taking responsibility for his own investments and he asked a businessman friend what advice he would give. Brad liked the answer.

'He said go buy yourself a good solid property, so that's how I got into the property side of things.'

He remembers his first transaction well.

'The first property. Yes I know it very well. It was a $269,000 house in my home town of Bay Village, Ohio. I fixed it up, and my mom and dad lived in it. We sold it for $330,000 about three years later. That was the first one I got into.

'So I said, "There's something in this". At first it was strictly a house I was buying back home for my mom and dad so that they didn't have any payments. That's how it started.'

A spark was lit. Brad had realized that property could be a great investment if you thought about it in the right way, and it had an element of the things he had enjoyed as a UCLA student: urban planning and architecture.

He soon found that he had something of a knack for it, and perhaps it was his goalkeeping instincts that had him considering all the angles, breaking down the variables and assessing probabilities. He evolved his own ideas on how to develop property, not based on a system of penalties, a term that goalkeepers hate anyway, but based upon shared incentives.

This is a reversal of normal practices and yet he is quite matter of fact about it.

'There are very easy ways to fix up a house at very minimal cost and make a profit on it. You get a builder that's very good and you work to split the profit on it.

'You could even split it 50:50 with him. He builds it at cost, you pay for the materials and you split the profit 50:50. That way you don't get stuck with crappy builders taking 25% or 30% rises on you, and hiding it in various places in the house.'

Brad's early experience with the financial adviser who still won out, even if the investments lost money, had taught him a lot. Now he was about creating win-win situations.

Turkish delight

After a spell in Denmark with Brondby, the UK work permit was still some way off and he signed a two-year contract to play for Galatasaray in Istanbul, Turkey. This was a good time to be in Turkey; the government had become alert to the prospect of joining the European Union and were beginning a strategy to lift the country's fortunes.

Brad was alert too. Alert to opportunity, as he remembers:

'In Turkey they were trying to open up trade in many different ways, for example tourism in places like Malvasia and Marmaris.

'They were offering one quarter acre plots for £30–40,000, which was very cheap. What you got was right on the ocean. Istanbul was always expensive especially round Torana and the Bosphorus. But there were other parts of Turkey where the weather is beautiful all year round, and they were really trying to attract people there.

'As a footballer I got lumps of money in periods. In Turkey you only got paid two times a year, so with a two-year contract I got four lump sums. So I started to think you have to do things to make your money work for you. So you could do this really safe route and put it in the bank or you could begin to play with some of it.'

———————————

So that's what he did, and it was successful. It established a good principle. Look for places where the land values were small and the potential was high. Combining this with his roving lifestyle, Brad has developed property in Turkey, Mexico and the USA.

A move to Columbus Crew, back home in Ohio, followed, before Liverpool finally secured a work permit and paid £1 million to take Brad into the Premier League. Even though he had two World Cup finals under his belt, he only made 30 appearances for the Merseysiders, before his former manager in Turkey, Graham Souness, took him to Blackburn Rovers.

Here Brad excelled as a professional, and really began to flex his muscles as a property developer. At the same time he was grateful for everything that football had given him and wanted to make a difference to other people's lives. An idea was being born.

Soccer in the US, unlike the UK, is primarily a middle class sport, and is much more popular than one would imagine. In fact, it is the second largest participation sport in the States. Brad began to work on a business plan. He wanted to find a way to reach kids in urban areas and inner cities, and to give them opportunities to fulfil their potential.

This was the start of what became Premier Soccer Academies. He says:

'Myself and my business partner got together and decided that to attract kids for scholarships we needed a facility. I came up with the idea of buying land at a cheap price and getting it re-zoned, doing due diligence with the government offices, and making a soccer academy out of it. We could generate income based on renting the fields. That's how it started.'

———————————

They began looking for a site. Brad realized that by now his name meant something in his local area and he did have a soft spot for it. Parts of the region are quite depressed and one hundred per cent tax breaks were being offered for investors.

This then creates the opportunity to go to the corporate sector and ask for investment and sponsorship, but Brad realized that you had to have more than just an idea.

'If you go and ask for a million dollars, you have to have something that they can feel and touch. So as this started evolving, this land sort of fell into our lap. It was a golf course which we bought at a very low price. We re-zoned it to take different uses and the land has nearly quadrupled in value. Now we have a lot of equity for development. We've taken 26 acres for our academy and we've got 32 acres of buildable land at the front.'

It is proving to be valuable frontage. Home Depot has just completed a 63 acre retail development just across the street, as part of the Lighthouse Village development comprising 400,000 square feet of retail space. The junction, which once coped with 12,000 cars a day, now has traffic of 30,000 cars a day.

This has done more than increase the value of the site: it has created interest in development for retail, hotels and commercial uses, and Brad is trying to secure a further 20 acres to extend the footprint of the site.

What a great piece of business, which came out of just trying to do some good. It has resulted in the construction of a $10 million soccer academy, the reclamation of underused land and the creation of jobs in an area where the blue collar workers have struggled since the closure of a local Ford Motor plant.

One thing feeds another, as a percentage of the profits from the commercial development project are endowed to the academy, which is a not-for-profit organization. Brad says:

'It's going to cost $1 million a year to run the academy, so we have to find this sum; otherwise it comes out of our own pocket.

'With the development up front we should more than be able to cover that. Then at the back in the academy we will be able to rent space out which should cover most of the basic costs, so that the endowment will be on top and allow us to make some advancements by way of scholarships. When you set it up as a non-profit, your goal is to have a bank balance of zero at the end of the year.

'So you could make investments, give scholarships, there's a million and one things you could do, but if you are always behind the eight ball it's hard. Of course there are repayments to be made. It's a $10 million project. The equity in the land takes it down to about $6 million that we have outstanding.'

So there is personal risk involved. He has taken personal responsibility to do something that he believes in and that he believes in time will realize investment growth. Yet it was the calculated risk of a goalkeeper.

'I didn't go into it blind, I went into it with my eyes wide open. I wouldn't have purchased the land if I didn't think I could win.'

To win on the commercial side means a good profit, and this in turn means a healthy academy. Brad is clear about what winning means in terms of the academy too, and it's not just about churning out soccer players.

'I want to genuinely give kids the opportunity to have experiences. It's not about giving them the life that I've had; everyone needs to lead their own way. The experiences that I have had have been absolutely invaluable. The third world countries where I've played soccer; see how they live their lives; see how they don't care about a television set; see how they don't care about the material things that they don't know about; they just get on with their lives. Those experiences outweigh anything.
'I'd like to give kids those kinds of experiences, through something they like which is football.'

He is excited that the academy is about reaching potential, and he says that everybody's potential is different; they may find the next David Beckham, but if not he has a clear philosophy:

'By the time a kid's eighteen, he may not make it as a footballer, but if he has given every last ounce of his effort, if he has reached his potential, within the football scheme of things, then we as an academy will help him out in any endeavour that he chooses to do. We can help him on a career path that he enjoys. That would be success for us.'

Team Friedel

Brad Friedel has proved himself to be a success on the football field; he is now showing the way to success off it. As a by-product, he is helping young people to define and create their own pathways to success. He is the first to admit that he hasn't done this on his own. He says:

'When I first started with the academy I was trying to do a little too much on my own – marketing, branding, for example, I've never done that before. That wasn't for me so I have hired an expert to kick-start that. I hired a gentleman from IMG to run the operational aspects of it. So I knew what I wanted to do, but I needed someone to pull in the reins a bit and say, "Great idea, next year. Let's do this now, these are the reasons". Then it would all fall into place. Being the decision maker, with someone else planning it, is an easier format for me.'

Soon, he will have a big decision to make: whether to continue in football as a coach, manager or even an owner, or whether to focus wholeheartedly on property development. He remains open-minded, saying that the only thing that he is certain of is that there will be frequent change, that he will not sit still and that he will do things that excite him.

What could be more exciting than performing at an elite level in front of thousands of people every week?

For Brad Friedel it seems that the answer is 'business'. He says:

'What does excite me is getting involved with the cities and the government in the inner cities; seeing a pile of dirt, knowing what I want to put on it and watch it grow in phases; watching the financial aspect of it grow. That excites me. That's nearly as good as walking out at Wembley.'

Entrepreneurial insights from the Rover

- Listen to advice, but take the advice that you believe in. Remember there are lots of advisers out there with nothing to lose. Brad found this when his investments lost, yet his adviser still won.

- Try to create incentives so that there is a win-win situation for collaborators. Trying to control things through penalizing people is time-consuming and may result in unpleasant surprises emerging down the line. Brad is happy to share profit with people who he can trust to pull in the same direction.

- Achieving social goals and being successful in business can go hand in hand. One can feed the other so that a symbiotic relationship is created and two plus two can equal six. Brad's proposals for a not-for-profit soccer academy were helpful in getting his site re-zoned. As a result, the value of the site has quadrupled, it will generate profits, and a proportion of these will help to keep the academy running.

- Whatever you do, be prepared for constant change and do things that excite you. Brad Friedel has had an exciting life as an Olympian and an elite athlete. If you create dreams and aspirations that are big enough and that you believe in, then watching piles of dirt transform into something else can be as exciting as walking out at Wembley – well, almost!

5

The Hustler

'These days I'm more interested in my animals than beautiful blondes.'

In the late spring of 1961 a new Act of Parliament came into force. The Gambling Act was to legalize off-track gambling in the UK. For the Hustler, it was a signal that he had been born into an opportunity. An opportunity which he was determined to grasp. He did.

Not just once; not even twice; but three times, and though he took possession of his bus pass a decade ago, who knows where the story will end?

Selwyn Demmy is a seventy-four year old multi-millionaire entrepreneur who still goes to the office seven days a week. Having sold three businesses for over £20 million, he is the man who has had more comebacks than Frank Sinatra. Over the years he has had a lot of media attention. He has been surrounded by the rich and the famous. This and his Midas touch in building one amazing business after another have focused attention on the glitz and the glamour.

All that this tells us is that he is an incredibly successful businessman. It tells us nothing of the person. Nothing of the mindset that seems to turn everything he touches to gold. To understand the person and get inside his mindset; to uncover the roots of his focus and determination, we must begin to understand the man, his life and how it has unfolded.

The man: the benevolent philanthropist, the connector, the market maker, and the voice of reason in a community which is barely big enough to accommodate all of its egos.

The Hustler first came into my consciousness some years ago, as the chap that came into the bar usually after ten o'clock. He would step out of a chauffeur-driven Rolls-Royce Phantom or a Bentley depending upon how the mood had taken him. Wearing a cashmere overcoat over his black tracksuit he would order a cup of Horlicks from his own jar which he kept behind the bar.

This was not some act of mean-mindedness. It was the mark of a man who, despite the trappings of wealth, and our expectations of millionaire bravado, has a simple philosophy. He is who he is and he is comfortable with it.

So, who is he? How has he managed to achieve dramatic business successes time and again? What drives his benevolence, his philanthropy and the maintenance of his huge, but loose, social network?

To find out we are going to have to look beyond the business pages and the Society section of Cheshire Life. We need to look at the man and his life. To do so, I am going to take you to a time and a place which for most of is difficult to imagine today.

Edward G., James Cagney and Humphrey Bogart all rolled into one

Gus Demmy, Selwyn's father, was one of six sons born into a tough environment on the northern side of Manchester. He worked his way from nothing to become an established bookmaker and subsequently a well-known boxing promoter.

He was a charismatic individual with a prolific appetite for business and an eye for style, always immaculately dressed. Selwyn recalls:

'He was a remarkable character. His favourite film star was Edward G. Robinson, and dad was Edward G., James Cagney and Humphrey Bogart all rolled into one. He was self made and came up from nothing.'

Gus married Sally and they had two sons, Selwyn and Harvey. They had high hopes for their sons and gave them both what they considered to be a good start in life; a boarding school education and an aspiration to become respectable professional types. In time, both were destined to become successful entrepreneurs. Selwyn says:

'Well, he didn't want me to be a bookmaker for starters. He wanted me to be all that he never had. Hence I went to university. I didn't like it. I wanted to get away from it.'

This theme of 'getting away' from the shackles that respectability had brought began even earlier in Selwyn's life. He was moved from one boarding school to another and never really found school to be a comfortable place. He still has today a letter that he wrote to his nanny imploring her to write a letter to the school, pretending to be his mum, requesting that he be taken out of school. He says he felt isolated and separate on account of being the only Jewish boy in school.

At one stage he ran away from school, but managed to complete his education and tried his level best to fulfil his parent's aspirations for him.

'I was articled to a firm called Charles Stone and Lawless in Moseley Street and at the same time I was taking my Intra LB at Manchester University. I went two years on the trot to try and pass it and didn't.'

His relationship with Gus became strained as Selwyn failed to live up to his father's expectations that he would become a member of the 'professional class'. This brought about a crunch moment, Selwyn remembers.

'I wasn't getting on too well with the fact that my father wanted me to be a lawyer. I was disappointing him too much. It was every self-made man's feeling of deliverance. The feeling that he had succeeded in making his son do what they call the 'right thing' in life.'

This was some pressure. It was not as though Selwyn didn't get on with his father. He admired and adored him. He so wanted to live up to his father's expectations, but his heart just wasn't in it. Worse still, he had become engaged, and he realized his heart wasn't in that either.

'She was a beautiful young lady that I didn't even like. I wanted to get away from that as well so I ran away from home.'

One night, aged twenty-one, he quietly packed his bag and slipped out of the house. Out of an unhappy situation and towards an opportunity. He does recall though that he left 'a very nice note' for his parents. He made his way to Liverpool and boarded one of the Isle of Man Steam Packet ships, arriving in Douglas ready to take on whatever life had to throw at him.

He turned up, suitcase in hand, at 25 Castle Mona Avenue, Douglas. He surveyed the sign above the premises. It said 'Mona Commission Agents'. This was the place. It was a telephone betting operation run by a friend he had come to know through his father. It was an unglamorous life, but Selwyn was hands-on, working in the office. Not trying to get to grips with obtuse principles of law, but observing the ebb and flow of something that was in his genes – the procedures and mathematics of professional gambling, something he had absorbed almost by osmosis as he had watched his father in action.

At last he had found something that he really enjoyed. It might not have been Gus's heart's desire for his son to want to go into his business, but at least there was some common ground. Selwyn arranged to come back and repaired the relationship with his parents. It was agreed that he would work for Gus, based at the track, but working on the telephone betting operation, just as he had done in the Isle of Man.

Gus had noticed something about his sons. He described Harvey as 'the diplomat': he was always good with people. Selwyn, he said, was 'the hustler', always looking for a deal. Meanwhile, 'the Hustler' was becoming alert to something that was happening in London …

Born into an opportunity

In Gus's heyday, gambling was illegal, unless it was conducted at the race track or over the telephone.

Of course telephones were not commonplace, and in poorer neighbourhoods, were virtually non-existent. The government had become concerned that the relative affluence enjoyed during the post-war 1950s had created a black market for gambling. Bookies 'runners' would collect stake money and deliver winnings, and much gambling business was being conducted in back alleys.

Clearly, there was no protection for the punter, and it had not gone unnoticed that the potential for tax revenues was being lost. Selwyn was alert to the fact that change was coming, and he was determined that, having been born into opportunity, he was not going to let this one pass him by.

In 1960, the government passed the Betting and Gaming Act. In October that year, the then Home Secretary, Richard Austen Butler, set up new Licensing Committees to consider applications from bookmakers to set up high street walk-in operations. Selwyn Demmy was out of the traps quicker than a White City greyhound. His was one of the first applications to be approved and in May 1961 he was officially in business.

He anticipated well, his speed of thought and willingness to act put him ahead of the game. Nobody really knew what the implications of the new Betting and Gaming Act would be. The 'big boys' in the gambling world hesitated. They imagined that betting shops would just be a small-scale concern which would simply give marginal backstreet activity a form of respectability.

They had not envisaged the cultural shift that high street betting shops would bring about. They were caught leaden-footed as betting shops began to open at the rate of 100 per week.

Selwyn realized that he was on to something. He opened his first shop on the third floor of a building at 53 Swan Street in Manchester. With just £200 and the help of a few friends, he fitted the shop out in just a couple of days. He still has very clear memories of how it felt.

> 'It took £72 in the first day, I remember the figure. It took two to three hundred pounds in each of the next five days. All the time, whatever you took, you kept some and gave so much back. The profit margin was such that it was obvious the potential was tremendous.'

He was off and running and his business instinct was insatiable. For him, night time was the right time. He trawled the streets of Manchester searching for locations for new shops. 'There's nothing like the midnight hour for weighing up sites for new shops', he fondly remembers.

Today, anyone looking for sites for betting shops, or any type of retail outlet for that matter, would key a series of demographic and economic variables into a Geographical Information System and wait an instant for it to tell you the optimal locations and the detailed characteristics of the constituent postcodes of the given neighbourhood.

Back in the early sixties you needed a tenacious approach to investigating locations; criteria for your search rested on human insight and the sharp instincts of a businessman for whom success had become an antidote. An antidote to the separation he had felt as a boarder at school; as a university misfit; as a son who had failed to live up to his parents' expectations and had exiled himself on a small island in the Irish Sea.

What's more it was visible success. Betting shops became much more prominent than the original room on the third floor in Swan Street. 'Demmy' signs were appearing all over Manchester. He was his own supercomputer, sifting and analysing the potential of one location after another, always looking for a frontline pitch where there was no other bookmaker. He says:

> 'I also looked at the pubs. Wherever there were pubs there were punters.'

His head start and his unrelenting approach meant that by the time the 'big boys' had realized that high street betting was going places, Selwyn had already arrived there.

He had been noticed and in 1982 Ladbrokes made him an offer he could not refuse. They took his chain of betting shops and in return gave him £6 million pounds. He didn't really think that they were worth it, so he took the money. He had an idea. An idea that had taken root as his social life had taken off.

The Blinker's years

Selwyn had become a well-known figure around Manchester. After all, every time you turned into a high street his name was staring you in the face. 'Demmy' signs seemed to be everywhere.

He also followed his father into boxing promotion, and worked with Jarvis Astaire to bring the big title fights to Manchester via closed circuit television and into Manchester's Odeon cinema. Selwyn's circle of friends began to include the rich, the famous and the influential. What's more, they were people who worked hard and played hard. A particular close friend was a young man from Belfast, who was causing quite a stir in the red and white of Manchester United. His name was George Best.

Before his death in 2005, Best recalled the night of the infamous World Heavyweight title fight between Sonny Liston and an up-and-coming young fighter called Cassius Clay, who later became a legend himself – Muhammed Ali. Best said:

'If you wanted to see a big heavyweight title fight live back then, the only way to do so was to stay up until the early hours and watch it at a big city cinema.

'Staying up until the early hours was, of course, never a problem for me and I definitely wanted to see that one. There was so much hype and excitement about that fight that it captured the imagination of everyone. So I was delighted when a Manchester bookmaker friend of mine called Selwyn Demmy organized a party which ended with us watching the fight at a cinema.'

By 1968, the Belfast Boy had helped Manchester United become the first English club to lift the European Cup, and that year he was voted the European Footballer of the Year and was awarded the Ballon d'Or, or Golden Ball. He and Selwyn had struck up a strong friendship.

When George was laid to rest after his untimely death, two photographs achieved prominence in the tributes paid by the *Manchester Evening News*. One was of George and Selwyn on holiday together in Majorca, taken in 1968. The other, also taken in 1968, was of a young boy waiting for his hero to sign his autograph.

The boy searched a lifetime for the photograph. Then in December 2005 he found it in the centrespread of the *Manchester Evening News*. They wanted to know who the boy in the picture was. We will hear more about him later in Chapter 13.

As for the other picture, a young Selwyn is seen with his friend holidaying in the sun. Both had the world at their feet, and a crowd of friends headed off to the sun.

They all spent a lot of time socializing in a Manchester nightclub owned by Tony Gordon, who was also the manager of pop star Lulu. Selwyn bumped into Gordon whilst in Majorca, and there was a friendly yet swift exchange of words. He recalls the events like this:

'I was in Majorca on the beach and Tony Gordon was there. He says, "Hello Selwyn", and we began talking and he says, "I'm thinking of going back to London". I said, "Good," Then jokingly said, "Why don't you sell me the club?" He said OK, we agreed a figure and shook hands. When I came back I went to the solicitors and bought it. That was 1968.'

In that moment on a beach in Majorca, the legend that was to become Blinker's nightclub was born. Over the next ten years you could have compiled a modern day version of '*Who's Who*' just by examining the guest list. It is a rare moment when Selwyn Demmy decides to blow his own trumpet, but for once, as he recalls the Blinker's years, he allows himself that little luxury.

'Anybody who was anybody whether it be Tom Jones, Lulu, you name it, pop stars of the day, everybody. I had that for ten years and sold it in '78. It was the best place … the most amazing club.'

If I may blow his trumpet a little more, regular visitors included George Best (of course); Miss World Marjorie Wallace; Michael Parkinson; Cliff Richard; Jimmy Saville; Olivia Newton-John; Jimmy Tarbuck; Alex 'Hurricane' Higgins; another Miss World, Belinda Green; Ian McShane; Michael Crawford; comedian Ken Dodd; and so the list could and does go on.

Selwyn was no stranger to the use of deadpan humour himself, especially when it helped him pursue his business goals and he was still busy building his bookmaking empire whilst Blinker's was at its height.

He was a master at generating publicity for his shops. When he rented a basement from a firm of solicitors in Chapel Walk, Manchester, he sat down and agreed with them his plans for making the basement into a betting shop. Perhaps not the best of his locations.

Part of the plan involved erecting one of his trademark blue and white 'Demmy' signs above the entrance. When the sign went up, the solicitors were horrified and said they had never agreed to it. They demanded that Selwyn take down the sign immediately.

He dug his heels in, convinced that he had an agreement. After four weeks of impasse, the sign was torn down, reportedly with a crowbar, and the *Manchester Evening News* covered the story. He replaced the sign, and put up a chalkboard offering odds on how the dispute would be resolved. He offered 4/6 that it would stay up; 11/8 that it would come down; and 5/2 that the dispute would be settled. He donated all the profits to charity, and threatened to camp outside the building to ensure that the sign didn't come down again.

As the weeks went by, more press coverage followed, almost on a weekly basis. Today, all he can remember of this comical episode is that he won the day and it was settled out of court. He says:

> 'I'll never know who took the sign down. All I know is I put it back up again.'

The upshot was that, because of all the media coverage, this less than ideal location was, for a long time, probably the most famous betting shop in the whole of Manchester.

Nothing lasts forever, and in 1978 Selwyn brought the Blinker's years to a close. Having engineered its fame, he swapped it for a fortune.

Those were great years. They gave him a taste for beautiful women, sparkling company and glamorous occasions. This was a sweet side dish to go alongside his real passion – work.

When, in 1982, Ladbrokes dropped £6 million pounds in his lap, the Blinker's years gave him an idea. He decided he would rather like to be a proper, full-time playboy. Monte Carlo beckoned.

An independent air

In the 1980s some 30,000 people lived in the 1.94 square kilometres that represents the Principality of Monaco. Enter number 30,001. Mr Selwyn Demmy, International Playboy.

Well, as the song says, he did 'walk along the promenade with an independent air, you could hear the girls declare he must be a millionaire'. Yet, surprisingly, he never did become the man who broke the bank at Monte Carlo. He didn't stay long enough, for a start.

His original plan was to go out there for three years and save the capital gains tax, then pick up the pieces of whatever he wanted to do. After only a few weeks, he realized that this playboy lifestyle was not for him. As a side dish, he had enjoyed it, but as a main course? He couldn't even contemplate the idea.

'I never thought I'd want to work again, with that kind of money in the bank, tax free. I could never spend the interest, let alone the capital. I thought this is the life for me.

'I was just not happy with my lifestyle because I didn't enjoy it there. Wine, women and song, you know, it was just one mad life, doing the things you think are wonderful, but you suddenly realize you've got nothing to back it up.

'You are not allowed to work because, to become a Monégasque citizen, you have to relinquish all your business rights; they were very keen on that in those days. I found that without work I was lost. I started drinking a lot and I suddenly realized that this wasn't the life for me.

'After the first two or three weeks I'd had enough, so I phoned up my accountant and said, "I'm coming home". He said "As long as you know what you are going to do." I said, "I'm going to pay my taxes", and as soon as I said that I felt better.'

Selwyn refuses to fly on account of his vertigo, so he sent for his old chauffeur who brought a Rolls-Royce down to Monaco. On the way back home across the rolling vineyards of France, he felt a tinge of excitement. He was heading back towards opportunity. He needed a challenge. Mentally he was rolling up his sleeves. There was work to be done.

Back to work

So the boy was back in town. And boy did he feel good about it. The big boys were all in the business now, but nobody knew how to find a good location better than Selwyn Demmy.

As well as his know-how, he had a name. One of his favourite sayings about the bookmaking business is 'if you haven't got a name you are not in the game'. He certainly had a name in this game. And he had considerable cash reserves, even after paying his taxes.

Selwyn was back in the saddle and he knew exactly what moves to make. The midnight hour was once again his happy hunting ground, and one betting site followed another. Ten years later he had 47 shops and Stanley Leisure approached him with an offer of £6 million to buy the lot. He took it and retired.

You guessed it. Retirement was short lived. He was bored and started again. Surely, he could not do it a third time. Yet his third chain was only six years old and 37 shops strong when Done came up with £10 million in 1998.

He took it and then declared:

'There will be no new empire building now. I've got my bus pass now. I've had my swan-song'.

He knew that working was not something that he had to do for money, it was something that he had to do for himself. It was part and parcel of his identity, of who he was and is.

In all of the deals he made, he never sold the Demmy name.

'I just wouldn't sell the name, but then in this industry they are buying you because they feel their name is better.'

You would think that a man with a bus pass and something like £50 million at today's prices would stop. But it is not about the money. He set up Demmy Credit, which is a credit and internet betting operation, and today, at 74 years of age, he goes to work seven days a week including most evenings.

He looks up with an expression of sweet resignation as he says:

'Unbelievable isn't it? I'm worse now than ever. I'm not ambitious anymore. I'm not looking for big things. I'm just going through the motions. If I wanted to go big again I could, all I've got to do is reinvest. In this business if you've got the name you're in the game, and all I would need to do is spend on advertising and staff and go bigger and bigger, but at my age who for and what for?'

He admits he has thought of selling off this business, but feels that he will go 'crackers' without it. When people ask him why he still goes to work, he has a stock answer.

'Sitting here talking to you is work. I go to the office because I enjoy it. If I didn't enjoy it, I wouldn't do it.'

King Midas to Dr Doolittle

The man with the Midas touch doesn't have many interests outside of business, but when he takes an interest in something, he shows a tenacity bordering on obsession, a characteristic of highly successful entrepreneurs.

For example, he has an interest in art. But in only two painters, L.S. Lowry and Arthur Delaney, both masters of the northern townscape of Manchester and Salford, the places where he grew up and made his success. He has arguably the world's foremost collection, owning something approaching half of Delaney's total output and frequently loaning Lowrys to Manchester's Lowry Centre.

His other interest is clocks and he has over 60, all kept in perfect working order and synchronized to the right time.

Then there are his animals. When he returned from Monaco, he heard about a property with potential in Cheshire. Knowing the owner, he knocked on the door and struck a deal there and then. He remodelled the house and began to enjoy the eight-acre gardens. So began his animal sanctuary.

'I used to get the odd phone call. It was a lady called June Wilmott, a particular friend of mine to this day. She runs her own animal sanctuary and she asked me if I could put the odd animal on my land, and then one more and two more and it just happened from there.'

Selwyn became something of a regular Dr Doolittle, and soon all kinds of waifs and strays were finding their way to Selwyn's home. He's even had goats tied to his gates. His dog kennels have to be seen to be believed, with underfloor heating, piped classical music and a large kitchen – The White Room – which has two washing machines especially for the dogs' blankets. He currently has seven dogs enjoying this luxury lifestyle.

Animal residents come and go and include Ginny, a dog that he rescued after she was thrown out of a car, and who has become a real performer. Once Selwyn got her on the road to recovery she couldn't stop singing and dancing for him. Soccer boss Graeme Souness rescued a dog on the streets of Lisbon after it was involved in an accident. As soon as he could, he flew it over to Selwyn's place where it recuperated. They called it Ben after Benfica, the team that Souness was managing at the time. Then, of course, there is the story of Leah and Bruno, two Great Danes found suffering from horrendous neglect. Leah was starving to death and was forced to eat two of her own puppies, whilst another four died at birth riddled with worms and fleas. Nobody imagined that they could survive, but one year on they approached the rest of their lives in reasonable health.

> 'It seemed only fitting that the two should live together in their own stable. They are an item now. They have been through the worst now they can get better as a couple.'

When Selwyn gave me his newspaper cuttings to look through, I was astounded. There were two piles. One was for his business cuttings detailing his remarkable life and career. One was for his animal stories. Both piles weigh about the same, and he is equally proud of them. These waifs and strays mean as much to him as his business successes, his playboy lifestyle and millions in the bank.

He explains how times have changed:

> 'I had three priorities in my younger days: making money, chasing ladies and looking after my animals. Now the last will be the first. Age gets to all of us. I started off dating beauty queens and finished up with old dogs and donkeys.'

He pauses to ponder the wisdom of his comments and adds:

> 'You give a dog a biscuit and he's happy. You give a lady a diamond and she wants another one.'

Inside the mind of a serial entrepreneur

Here we have a fascinating and inspirational tale of a driven man, obsessive, tenacious and yet heart-warmingly philanthropic. A man who has always had a feeling, as entrepreneurs inevitably do, of separation, of being different, of not meeting expectations in their early years.

It is the determination to shed these feelings of separation that creates the unshakeably powerful focus and the feeling of not being able to give up because to give up brings about the fear of being separate in some way.

Here we have a man who has never had family of his own. He says:

'I bought three engagement rings, but never made it to the altar.'

Yet the concept of 'family' seems important to him.

He maintains a very large network of loose friendships, many stretching right back into his childhood.

Then of course he has his animals. Not just any animals: animals that know that feeling of separation, whether through neglect, cruelty, rejection or just because they were somehow different. These are the kind of animals that he has a real affinity with. Animals that, if they were humans, would have every reason to become entrepreneurs.

Entrepreneurial insights from the Hustler

- You don't have to go far to make your fortune – Selwyn stayed on his home turf, apart from a brief sojourn in Monaco, an attempt to live the 'millionaire dream' that backfired. Detailed knowledge of his patch and his people made him the best site-finder in the business.

- If you know it, use it – Selwyn was born into the betting business. He absorbed the knowledge almost by osmosis. But, crucially, he used what he knew, and developed and built on it to render the business agile and responsive to a changing world.

- The power of reputation. You must build your own personal brand and brand values – As Selwyn says, 'In this business, if you haven't got the name you are not in the game'. It's actually the same in most businesses: you must cultivate your reputation, believe in what you stand for and be consistent.

- If you are good at something and find something that suits you, then do it, do it again, and again – why stop at once? Selwyn built essentially the same business three times, selling them off for more money each time. Staying in the same sector can pay off. It is not unusual for entrepreneurs who have succeeded in one sector to try their hand in another sector and lose their shirt. Very few entrepreneurs succeed when they cross over into another type of business.

6

The Undertaker

'I thought, "How am I going to make my mark? Time is not on my side" – I was nineteen years old.'

The Moroccan guys pulled up alongside Mike Cooper's Citroen 2CV, which he'd bought with the proceeds of a summer spent selling drinks on a beach in the South of France. They wound down their windows to speak, and Mike smiled. The Moroccans didn't smile back; they didn't look as though they were in holiday mood. They warned Mike to stop trading, it was their beach and they said they had the rights to it.

Mike reasoned with them. He politely explained that he had looked into it and no permits were issued for beach trading. The Moroccan disagreed. He reached down into the glove compartment, pulled out a gun and fired. BANG.

Unhurt but unhappy, Mike reasoned that it was near the end of the season, and the sensible thing would be to return home. His French phrasebook had been useful, but it was no match for a pistol.

Yet he had tasted something that he liked. The lad from Bolton had realized that there was a big world out there full of amazing things. What he didn't fully appreciate was that he had a way with people that made him a natural-born salesman. He had a feeling that he was destined for a life as an entrepreneur, but quite how, he had yet to figure out.

Today, he is a likeable and unassuming gentleman who doesn't carry around an outsized ego. He is the kind of person that you would like to help. Not that he needs much help these days. His company, Avalon Trustee, which sells funeral policies, has clocked up £17 million in policy income, has an actuarial surplus of 135%, is expanding across the globe and has an exciting property portfolio.

More overtaker than undertaker

Of course, Mike is a million miles removed from any undertaker. The name just sort of stuck. We go to the same health club and one of the members can never remember anyone's name. He knew that Mike did funeral policies and so whenever he was referring to him he would say, 'You know who I mean – the undertaker'.

In fact Mike is more of an overtaker than an undertaker. When he really got into the swing of things and found he had a natural talent he overtook just about everybody in sight and became the number one salesman in Europe. His is another incredible tale, yet you would never know it, he would only tell you if asked. Not because he is secretive, but because he is quite modest.

I remember, as my children were growing up, one of my often-repeated mantras to them was, 'Good things happen to good people'. As the years go by and things happen, one sometimes begins to doubt the validity of this piece of homespun wisdom.

Meeting Mike Cooper is enough to restore one's faith that good things do in fact happen to good people. He oozes goodness. Not in a smarmy way, but in a down-to-earth, genuine way which is backed up by his beliefs and behaviours.

He frequently talks of doing the right thing; being fair; the importance of friendship; family; responsibility; and trust. He started out with a natural advantage – his amiable manner and modesty means you just cannot help but like him. He added to that an insatiable appetite for learning and taking advice – he systematically cultivated his own luck – and work. Boy, does this fellow have an appetite for work.

Yet somehow he comes out of it as a well-balanced family man, and one of the first things he says to me is:

> 'They say behind every successful man is an unspoken hero – your wife or partner. I've known Clare since I was 17, and a great deal of my success does come through Clare. WE are successful. Every part of my success is hers.'

I told you that you would like him.

Small things, big difference

It is hard to know what created the intense drive and work ethic that lies behind Mike Cooper's success. Unlike most entrepreneurs, he came from a stable and loving family and didn't, as far as he is aware, experience deep feelings of being an outsider, often the hallmark of the entrepreneur. All that he does remember is a positive feeling that he was different. He says:

> 'I guess I can remember doing things that were different from other people without thinking about it. We had a great family background. We didn't have much but we didn't want for anything. We didn't have much money.
>
> 'I had to find ways and means of having the things I wanted. I remember at ten years old having a sale of some stuff to go and buy a gun that I wanted. I remember caddying twice a day on Sunday as a young lad carrying huge golf clubs on my shoulders around links golf courses. Walking 8 or 9 miles for 50p a time.
>
> 'I'd get £2 for that and I bought this £18 gun that should have been £36. So I got a gun. It was probably better than other people's guns at the time but I got it through hard work.'

So it was, perhaps subconsciously at this stage, that Mike Cooper began laying the principles which would allow him to build an empire. It was the idea that small things like 50p's could transform into something big if you worked very hard.

He did work very hard. It is what he has always done. Perhaps that is a bit of an understatement. He has a capacity for work which is more than above average; it is exceptional.

He remembers how his working life started, leaving school at sixteen without any qualifications.

> 'I did all sorts of things, whether it was labouring or menial work. I'd work up to being an unqualified success at The Last Drop in Bolton, running the bistro at the age of nineteen.'

It was here that another of the things that have influenced Mike's career began to happen. People in positions of power have tended to notice that he is different, and have liked what they have seen.

One day the General Manager asked to see Mike. He was astounded to find that Mike was earning more than the Head Chef. He asked Mike, 'What are you doing?' His response was simple. He said:

> 'It's just the hours I work. I was always very happy to work 15 or 16 hours every day, seven days a week. I was always interested in the work. I wanted to learn, to apply myself.'

He knew that if he wanted to work he had to be there and he would walk three miles a day in each direction often in his wellies to make sure he was there. Nights shifts, day shifts – any shifts – were not a problem; he simply took an interest in what he was doing and applied himself to an extraordinary degree. Yet, as far as Mike was concerned, it was not extraordinary. He had simply decided that he would apply his own standards.

'I knew then that other people's limitations bear no resemblance to mine. I would be happy to put myself through whatever was required to achieve whatever I needed to.'

Brass bands, barriers and bodies in beds

An attitude was forming. An attitude that said you could do anything you wanted to; if you had the desire and the application; and that barriers are there to be broken down.

When Mike heard that a friend was going on tour to Holland with his brass band, he liked the sound of it and thought he would quite like to go. For most people, the fact that they could not play a note on a musical instrument would be enough for them to dismiss this as a fanciful idea. Yet Mike got himself made band librarian, looking after the music, a job that he could do whilst sampling a new culture.

The different culture was a real eye-opener for him, he was having a ball, and his taste for the good times even got him into the public eye. He laughs as he remembers the set-up.

'We were all with exchange families to get to learn the culture. I was with a younger family. Their son was fifteen and I was quite a bit older. I wanted to have a few drinks and explore the life.

'They have this lovely way of doing the drinks in Holland. You have this big old wooden spoon to wipe the froth off your pints. It's strong stuff. One night I had too much to drink. Everyone rode on bikes; it was really nice. I was staying in this top floor room. I got back and parked the bike. All the lights were off in the house and I thought, "Well OK, I'm going to get in trouble here". After you have had a few you rationalize things. I climbed up the drainpipe onto the balcony on the top floor, opened the door quietly and collapsed onto the bed. Two bodies jumped up. I thought, "Jesus what's that?" I was in the next-door neighbour's bed. He jumped up and was chasing me around the room.'

The story hit the headlines in Holland. Interestingly, other than this you won't find very much printed about Mike Cooper, which is extraordinary given what he was about to go on to achieve.

The tour ended and a few people decided to hitch-hike to the South of France. Of course, Mike couldn't be idle. He bought a drinks cooler, stocked up with drinks and doughnuts and began to sell to customers on the beach. Pretty soon there were ten people working on a seven-mile stretch of beach, and they were doing well. That is, until the intervention of the Moroccan helped Mike to understand the value of a tactical withdrawal.

In Chapter 5 we heard how Selwyn Demmy had become disenchanted with his life in Monte Carlo, and had driven home through the vineyards of France, mentally rolling up his sleeves and preparing for another challenge. He was in a Rolls-Royce and he knew exactly what he was going to do.

By contrast, on that same stretch of road, a young Mike Cooper was travelling in less salubrious conditions, not knowing what he was going to do, just knowing that he had to do something. He had to make his mark. He remembers the feeling quite clearly.

'I was really anxious. Very anxious about making my mark and doing something. I remember that vividly. It was a long journey home. I was writing lots of notes about different things – what I could do and how I could do it. I was thinking then that time's not on my side. I was only nineteen. I was thinking, "I've got to get going".'

He arrived home like a coiled spring waiting to be unleashed. He didn't have to wait long for his chance.

Beach shorts to bonuses

Almost immediately an acquaintance suggested he come for an interview with a financial services company. So he went right away, still wearing his beach shorts and a dirty shirt.

Today, he speaks in total wonderment about that interview, as if he has only just returned from it and it has not quite sunk in. The man at the interview gave Mike a glimpse of what might be. He says:

'He was funny. He said, "In this company you can earn a lot of money". He said, "You could earn so much, you see that video over there, you could just go and buy that, cash".

'I said, "You are joking – that would be £500, just like that?" I said, "That's fantastic". He had a lovely shiny BMW outside and I thought, "Wow, look at that". So I thought, "That's for me, that sounds great".'

He saw something in Mike. Even though he was too young to be bonded, he took him on and sent him for training. For Mike, the quality of the training and the American way of doing things were a revelation. He felt comfortable, too. His attitude was that as long as he was ethical and not doing any harm to anybody then he was willing to do it. When they explained that the company founder was a self-made man who went from a nickel and a dime to being worth $400 million, some were cynical. Mike's attitude was different.

'I thought this sounds just like me, or what I think is me. My vision of me. So I went to work for them very young as a spotty teenager. I did very, very well with them. European salesman of the year. I did things that very few other people would do again. I was a natural at it.'

The best in Europe out of 3000 salesmen, and still only twenty-two. What was he doing? Partly the answer was the same as the answer he gave when asked why he was earning more than the Head Chef. He was working long and hard. In addition, he was hungry to learn and always sought advice and guidance. Thirdly, he has an intuitive knack for making his own luck.

He quickly understood the variables that created opportunities and sales, and his instinct was to maximize every attribute. Firstly, he would employ good sales-manship skills, something that he had a natural aptitude for, so it didn't seem forced. Secondly, he would sell multiple products to clients rather than just one. Thirdly, he would seek referrals, and sell multiple products to people he was re-ferred to. Other salesmen did this too, but in the whole of Europe, no one did it to the intensity of Mike Cooper.

The financial rewards were huge, and he enjoyed them, yet he maintained the presence of mind to use them as both motivation and payback, so that he never hit a comfort zone. He just kept getting better and better. He says:

'I loved the Porsche, I loved the other things and I knew about them early. So at twenty-three I bought my first fast car – a 944 Turbo – having set myself a goal at the start of the year that very few people believed.

66

'I set it out in a detailed format, that within 6 months I would save up £18,000 buy a car at double the value, and that was at 23. In six months, but that was a by-product of my career ambitions, that was a payback to reward my motivation of doing well in business. One has to balance the other. You have to – Ying and Yang, isn't it? You have to have a balance between what you do in business and a payback.'

Six months later, Mike arrived home with a brand new £35,000 Porsche. His wife Clare was aghast. She said, 'Christ, what have you done?' Yet Mike is quite clear why he had to go and buy it. Sure, he loved the car, but it was about following through. Doing what you say you are going to do. A principle which has stood him in good stead ever since.

This was at a time when Mike's friends were driving Ford Fiestas and doing normal things. He recalls pinching himself when he drove that Porsche. He didn't rest on his laurels, he began to do something that would become another trademark behaviour – reinvestment. He got into property before the boom.

The bonuses continued to be great and, inevitably, Mike was the regular star at the annual bonus-giving ceremony. Yet it was one of these events that slightly unsettled him and got him thinking along another track.

The bonus handouts were always a big occasion. One year everyone knew that one particular salesman hadn't done too well, so it was a surprise when the President called him up to the front. 'So', said the President, 'Tell us what you *didn't* do this year'. Then he handed the salesman a giant-sized cheque and, where the amount should have been written, it said 'Joker'.

Mike didn't like the public humiliation. He was doing well, at the top of the tree, but he realized that one day that could be him. He started to realize that he was income wealthy but capital poor.

The next year at the bonus ceremony, he was invited to the front by the President who announced with a flourish, 'Here's a guy that won't be leaving here in a hurry. Come on up for your £18,000 bonus. Mike Cooper, another record year.'

In the back of Mike's mind he knew that his future lay somewhere else.

Breakdown in communications

It did, and he walked out of his £100,000 a year job on good terms to go and do something else. Something he knew nothing about: a telecoms start-up, with no salary unless he could earn it.

It was the idea of a friend who was so taken by Mike's sales abilities that he invited him to become the major shareholder. In Mike's mind that was flattering, but he preferred fairness, and they agreed on a 50:50 split.

The timing was good. It was the start of the digital telephone systems that could reroute calls for least cost. The trouble was that there was only one provider at the time, Ferranti. This didn't deter Mike and his partner. Even though they were a start-up business, they convinced Ferranti that they were the people to take on the regional dealership. They took off very fast, as Mike recalls:

> 'For the first year we did £750,000 worth of business. We were selling telephone systems.
>
> 'It was either a one-off sale as a purchase or we would set up a lease. We could play with the leasing rates to get a higher fee, so we weren't just selling the phone system but also the financial rate. I learned there that small financial adjustments at one level could have huge bottom-line repercussions.'

The business took on half a dozen sales people and a support infrastructure and it was going well. Then, for Mike, something intuitively didn't feel right. When he put some analysis alongside this feeling he saw it: the pipeline of possible orders was growing, but the business they were winning was shrinking. Huge interest rates had made financial directors much more cautious and they were just not buying the product.

He then had to do one of the most difficult things in his life. He sat down with his colleague, his friend, and said, 'If this business carries on it is going to be bankrupt. It can't support my objectives in where I expect the business to be.'

> 'I thought, "Crikey that's not you, why are you doing this carry on?" But I thought it's not right. I have to draw a distinction between business and pleasure – this is business.'

It was difficult because of the friendship, but also because his colleague's parents both worked in the business, so Mike handed over his shares and walked away with nothing.

Bouncebackability

He was twenty-nine, now with a young son, two mortgages and a car loan. He needed £3000 a month just to stay afloat.

Leaving somewhere on good terms is a good idea. It meant he could go back into financial services and buy himself some thinking time. He moved to a competitor for a big package and got a surprise. 'I fell flat on my face', he says.

The corporate culture suffocated him. He felt unable to exercise his own instincts and was hidebound by systems, procedures and the judgements of those higher up the corporate ladder.

Instead he felt something he had never felt before.

'I felt like a failure. On the face of it I was a successful person, but inside I didn't feel successful. Wanting to advance myself, I thought I had … I had unfinished business.'

Reflection can be a powerful teacher, and now Mike was able to reflect not just on success, but also on failure, and he began to have a few thoughts that were to come together when he took on a salesman, one who proved to be a bit out of the ordinary.

'I knew we had missed out in the telecoms business because of the one-off nature of the sales. I thought, when you do right by somebody, if you can complete a financial arrangement and maintain an ongoing relationship, you can still be earning from it years down the line.

'I thought, whatever it is, I want to be involved in something that is small in cost and which renews. I didn't have a clue what it was.'

Ever since the days of saving small amounts to buy a gun, he had always liked the concept of small things growing and taking on a cumulative effect. He had noticed how remarkable it was that people in the financial services sector could not be bothered with what seemed like small things. He says:

'We had targets for direct debit renewal. Very few people bothered. They earned 10% of the premium by putting people on direct debit. So if you put £149 on DD you would earn £1.49, but I knew that if you put 100 people on DD you would earn £14.99, if you did 1000 it was £149. Not just for that month; it was ongoing, cumulative. When I left, the total value was £14,500 a year from other people not being bothered. If I could do something like that I could put my feet up. That's working smart.'

Then in through the door walked a young man called Nigel Waugh. Mike remembers him well.

'He always seemed to look good, drunk, a real party animal, the toast of Cheshire. I was intrigued by him. He came to work with me. Boy was he a grafter. He would be on calls at 9.30 at night.'

Nigel was very bright, but had left university after just seven weeks. He was very family orientated, and even through his ups and downs, always tried to look after his mother and brother. Mike remembers him as unpredictable.

'He was always close to the edge. He bought this house and he would sell the kitchen out of it, to try and get some money for something else. Then one minute he is sleeping on his brother's floor. He was a real up and down guy.

'But he was always a very funny guy and always saw the bigger picture. When we were reading a financial services handbook he was reading a book on mergers and acquisitions – at twenty-one years old. He had nothing at all.

'Subsequently he built up the second biggest debt recovery insolvency business in the UK, Gregory Pennington, which I helped him fund. Then he built up Eurocall, a telecoms company with 20,000 business customers. He sold that for £30 million and retired at forty.

'I saw a lot of similar traits in Nigel. The difference was, though he was very clever, he didn't care about human emotions. I am about build and grow – save and prosper.'

Yet Nigel had an off-the-wall idea that got Mike thinking. He said, 'Why don't we think about funeral plans?' At first the idea was greeted with distaste. When Mike researched the market he found that the key players were turning over millions of pounds. How? Nigel's response was, 'Think about it. It's just like a life policy.' For Mike, that was one of those 'aha!' moments. He thought:

'Hold on, a life policy is a death policy but with a different name. It's not the thing; it's how it's perceived. I thought, 'Wow, at the moment it's morbid but if you change the way it's marketed it could be perceived to be positive".'

That began the idea that became Lifecare, which is really a funeral services policy by another name. But it wasn't that simple. Remember, this is Mike Cooper.

'I had to do the right thing. Whatever I've been involved with, I can stand up tall and look anybody in the eyes. And they would know about me and what I stood for.'

He had to do it properly. An approach which meant he had to spend five years and £250,000 setting it up. He had to set up a top class trust fund and needed advice that no local solicitor could give. He needed a bank to front it. Banks just don't fund start-ups, but Mike's incredible ability to sell himself combined with an idea, plus great references from people he'd worked with, resulted in Barclays putting their name on his brochure from day one.

He started the process of setting up in 1990, and because of its complexity and the need to do it right, the first plan was sold in November 1994. He remembers it well, to the point that he can tell you the names and addresses of the people who bought the first plans, and the salesman who sold the first one. That salesman is still with the company at the age of 73.

People do tend to stay with Avalon Trustee, Mike's company, because there is this feeling of being wanted. It's rather like a family. Mike brought with him the people ethos that he thrived on in his early days in financial services.

'Even today, I say to people funeral plans is a by-product of what we do. We are a people company; we are about developing our people: their sales potential, their livelihoods and their path in life.

'We are about enhancing people's lives. The core theme now is to have ten millionaires work for the company, that's our big thing. It's not about Mike Cooper; it's about other people.'

Now policy income is in the region of £17 million, behind which is a trust fund with an actuarial surplus of 135%. What this means is for every £1 that Avalon is required to invest on behalf of a policyholder, the company actually invests £1.10. This small additional sum enjoys compound growth over long periods of years, ensuring that Mike can sleep at night knowing that every policyholder is more than provided for. The investment income from managing this trust also creates a profit centre for Avalon, which has to compete with its other profit centres selling policies in the UK, Spain and now USA.

Whereas funeral plans were traditionally aimed at lower socio-economic groups in the UK – a functional purchase aimed at those least likely to be able to afford a proper funeral, they have expanded significantly because of the growth in expatriates living abroad. They want peace of mind that they will be flown home and be given a decent send off – this is now a lifestyle purchase for the more affluent, and is proving to be a boom market.

Avalon invests trust funds in a range of investments, and Mike has been able to develop his interest in property, and enjoy the intellectual challenge of trying to read the business cycles in order to move money between domestic and commercial property, the stock market, deposits and bonds. Though the trust fund is very successful and the surplus could be drawn down, not one single penny has been.

'I believe in growing organically; we don't have a penny of loan or overdraft. I believe in the sales dynamic. If we don't sell we don't eat.'

Despite the success, Avalon remains a hungry, growth-orientated outfit which has a small team of ten key people. People who, if they achieve the challenging growth plans that have been set out, will, with Mike's blessing, all become millionaires in their own right.

With such a sound and stable platform, Mike has the presence of mind to think about what he really wants out of life. He is now beginning to shift to focus from working in the business to working on the business. The idea of taking things a bit easier resulted in him buying a property in Switzerland which he is renovating at present.

As so often happens when entrepreneurs take up a hobby, they cannot help but turn it into a business. He has become friends with the largest landowner in the area and plans to buy all the land around his chalet.

'Then I can develop a resort, a ski resort, a lifestyle resort, because a lot of people don't like skiing but they like being there.'

As the resort idea develops, his focus on Avalon remains intense. He lives and breathes growth. When he met with his ten key players in La Manga, they got a surprise: Mike had set the table for twelve people. He explains:

'We had the best ever meeting in La Manga. It was ten people but it was set out for twelve. I said, "There's going to be twelve people at the next meeting. Two people we don't even know, now isn't that exciting? We are getting excited about those two people we don't even know, and they haven't even been interviewed yet".'

He's proud of the past and excited about the future. He feels he's been lucky, worked hard and looked after people.

'Every opportunity seems to bring another glimpse through another window. Somebody told me once to make your vocation your vacation. That's what I do. Everything I do is enjoyable. Whether it's speaking to someone who's not doing well or cutting a deal on a Ferrari, I enjoy it.

'My psyche comes from my parents, lovely people. We like to think of people as family. Be normal. The psychological business aspect of that is that people perform better if they are relaxed.'

I rest my case. Good things do happen to good people.

Entrepreneurial insights from the Undertaker

- Set your own standards – Mike Cooper broke the mould because he didn't allow norms to dictate his standards or his beliefs about what was possible. Set yourself the standards that you believe are right for you. Set higher standards.

- Work hard – Unless you have some extraordinary and exceptional talent, hard, focused work is an essential ingredient of entrepreneurial success.

- Don't rule out things that have a small price tag associated with them. The world's most profitable companies sell small things a lot of times; if you can combine this with compound growth as Mike has done, you could really be onto something.

- Do the right thing – You get out of life and business what you put in. Be clear about what you stand for and behave ethically – even when you have to do difficult things. When you need help and support, people will always back you up if you have done right by them.

7

The Prince

'Never ever, ever, ever, give up. Ever.'

Standing at the highest point of Alderley Edge, the Prince stared down into the darkness. In the blackness below lay a 500 foot drop down a rugged sandstone escarpment that rises up from the Cheshire Plain. He drew heavily on his Columbian cigar. He tried to clear his head. His business troubles weighed heavily on his shoulders. Everything was collapsing around him and it seemed there was no way out. Or was there?

Again, he stared into the abyss that lay below him. In the distance he could see the bright lights of Manchester, the place where, as a boy, he had dreamed of glory. It reminded him of the faces of his two young children.

He drew on his cigar again. There was a way out. This was not it.

He decided that in business and in life you should 'never, ever, ever, ever give up. Ever.'

More than just 'Duked'

Albert Edwards is a larger-than-life character. It is the only way to describe him. He is charismatic, flamboyant, hilarious, unpredictable, unconventional, dapper and charming. It is true, where business is concerned, that he can be incisive – some might even say ruthless. Yet he can be kind and thoughtful. In the course of just one sentence he can be both inspirational and idiotic. They only made one Albert Edwards and that is the greatest compliment I can give.

Selwyn Demmy, 'the Hustler' we heard about in Chapter 5, is the Elder Statesman of our community. He is respected.

You will recall that Selwyn has a love of animals, most especially those on the margins. I've noticed that he is this way with people too. He watches for those on the margins. I was with him once when he was explaining how a particular person had come into the village, alone, unusual, not quite fitting in. Selwyn had taken the trouble to be seen in the company of this person often. The effect of this in a small village, believe it or not, was to give the person credibility, so that despite his social unease, people began to accept him. He had been 'duked' so to speak.

Albert Edwards, by contrast, has such a magnetic personality that he could not be on the periphery if he tried. Instead, Selwyn has given him a unique honour and bestowed upon him the title of 'Prince' Albert.

Partly, it is a reference to Selwyn's brief sojourn in Monaco where the real Prince Albert was on the throne. Partly, it is an appropriate title for someone who has an aristocratic air and, when he wants to be, can be a regular Prince Charming.

He has gone from pauper to prince. We were born little more than a mile apart on exactly the same day: 11th May. That is the bit of our birth date that I have the responsibility for remembering. Albert, being good at figures, has the responsibility for remembering which year. Neither of us minds too much that his head for figures is not what it used to be.

His life has been a rollercoaster ride. He lost everything, which enabled him to find something. Something important. He found out who his real friends are. Now he is back on a roll again.

It all began in Manchester's Moss Side, where his Jamaican mother filled his head with images of the grand life that she had left behind and told him something that became ingrained in his beliefs and behaviours.

She told him he was 'special'.

The roots of a prince

Born into a family of six children, Albert was the only son. His mother came from a high-ranking black family in Jamaica. Her father was Chief of Police. She had a choice of going to the United States or to England and she chose the latter. She fell in love with Albert's father, fell pregnant, and that was that. That was how it was in those days.

Albert's father worked hard and developed a haulage business. Not spectacular, but it fed and clothed them. Albert knew from an early age that his mother was a bit special, perhaps in a different league. He recalls an incident that only made sense to him many years later, long after his mother had died, and when he had some experience of life. He sees it like this:

'You know in life when you are a boy, you have lots of different experiences – you take a lot of things in don't you? It's not until later in life it becomes clear what it was.

'I remember being at the front door tugging on my mother's skirt. The door opens. I remember this older gentleman. He had a black suit, tie, handkerchief in his top pocket, an official car outside. It was Sir Clifford Campbell. He was Governor General of Jamaica, appointed by the Queen. My mother's father was the Chief of Police in Jamaica. I remember she used to tell me that she had servants and people that brushed her hair.

'They were a well-known family. She came here looking to do something different. Then she met my father and that was it. She got pregnant with me and got married because that's the way it was. I'm the oldest.

'I remember the look on my mother's face. When I got older I realized what it was. I remember him looking at her and her looking at him. He knew what her family was and where she'd come from – and she knew. To see her in the circumstances that he found her in. There was a reaction between the two of them.'

Albert was a quiet boy, growing up surrounded by his mother, whom he adored, and his five sisters. His mother was educated and a music teacher, so the house was always full of people. People would come from Jamaica to start a new life and rent a room. Others would come because Albert's mother taught piano, she was literate and would read and write letters for people and represent them. With all the comings and goings, Albert was becoming an astute observer of people.

One of the first black teachers in the whole of Manchester was a man called 'Teacher' Brown. He grew up in Jamaica with Albert's mother and would ride his bike to the house. It was a difficult time for him. He encountered racial prejudice, not just from his pupils, but from his colleagues as well. His troubles were forgotten when he visited the Edwards household. He would bring with him photographs of where they had grown up. Images of large, five-bedroom houses, kidney-shaped swimming pools, and servants. It was a different world. A world that Albert had never known, but a world that he felt he had a right to be part of. He says:

'That just indoctrinated me. I was brought up to be … she used to say to me "you are special. You've got five younger sisters. I worry about you because one day you will have to bring up a family".'

These simple evenings spent reminiscing over old photographs were mesmerizing for Albert. He would sit and listen, dreaming that he would be a part of it.

Dreaming of glory. He has told me many times of the effect this had on him. He says:

> 'The things you do as a child are important. The things you are exposed to are important. I remember being at school and the teacher said to everyone, "How do you see yourself when you are twenty five?"
>
> 'That seemed ancient, and everyone said the predictable things. I said, "Well, I see myself being married with five children and living in a detached house with five bedrooms and two bathrooms."
>
> 'I looked at everyone and they were laughing at me and I said, "Well, my mother always had two bathrooms." Everyone just looked at me. I was motivated by things like that.'

And so it is that in this great future you can't forget your past. On many occasions Albert and I have sat up into the early hours – two boys born on the same day, same month, same year and for all we know, possibly the same moment – talking about the influence of events in our early years.

There is one story of Albert's that I like in particular. His mother was a member of the Upper Room. It was an elite Christian society comprised mostly of business people and intellectuals. One particular couple, stalwarts of the Upper Room, an academic and his bohemian wife, took a shine to the family. This is something that Albert has never forgotten and which he speaks about with genuine and deep emotion.

> 'We used to go to a gathering at the Airport Hotel or somewhere – we were the pepper on a white sand beach and the people were really nice. We had a friendship with Vicky and Professor Harris. Vicky was American, she was an artist and she used to come to the house.

> 'They were really down-to-earth people. When I look back now, I admire them even more. We had such a simple home and Vicky used to borrow clothes mum had made. They used to go around together, very humble. I remember going to Hartley Road in Hale where they lived. I could swear that the front door was massive, walk down the drive and this massive wooden front door confronted you. For years in my mind it was massive, until one day when I was successful, I went back and it didn't seem that big and the house didn't seem that big.
>
> 'But what I remember is that it is amazing how people can be so kind.'

Sitting at his mother's feet he could dream his dreams of glory; he could be, as she said, 'special'; he could bask in the warm kinship of the Upper Room.

Yet beyond these beautiful moments life was hard. He could not help but feel different – after all he was 'special'. But the difference, the feeling of separation, was all around him.

He was a black boy in a predominantly white world; he was the only boy amongst five sisters; his grandiose dreams of the future set him apart from his classmates. These things alone are reasons enough to set the scene for entrepreneurial growth and success. Yet for Albert there was more separation to come.

Greased nipples and dirty nails

We have yet to talk about Albert's father. Like most men of his day he was busy working. He had a small haulage business. Each day, before Albert went to school, he had a job to do on his dad's hydraulic trucks. He was responsible for greasing the nipples. He didn't mind so much because sometimes he got to drive the trucks around the yard.

But he had his mother's genes, he liked flamboyance, style and grooming. It used to irritate him that greasing the nipples left dirt under his finger nails and he would scrub with Swarfega and use a pin to try to scratch them clean.

In the evenings his father would come home and introduce Albert, at the age of eight or nine, to his evening job. He recalls:

'How we made money is that we knew the weight of the truck, laden and unladen. So the rates vary depending on the material carried. My job was to work out the cost per load and how much people were to pay him. That was my job.

'Eventually I got 100% in mathematics because of that experience. Then there was a point when I really cottoned on and I started to play the numbers. I realized that you could bill a bit more by adjusting the calculation – not by too much, you had to spread it.'

When his father was able to afford a Ford Zephyr, Sundays would often involve a drive out to Cheshire to admire the big houses. Albert sat quietly, but he was beginning to develop an interest in property, dreaming his dreams that one day, one of these Cheshire mansions would be home.

Having developed a work ethic from an early age, he always did part-time jobs. He saved. He longed to have nice things. In fact, he would rather have one nice thing than lots of things that he regarded as tacky.

Then one day he had saved enough cash to buy the object of his dreams: a used Ford Cortina. The lacklustre colour though didn't appeal to his flamboyant tendencies. He did what anyone would do – he had it painted aubergine. The boy in the aubergine Cortina had hit the streets. Not surprisingly, he was getting noticed.

Then things took a turn for the worse. The Victorian house in Moss Side was compulsorily purchased, and they bought a three-bedroom place in Stretford. One bedroom for mum and dad, one bedroom for Albert and one for all five sisters squeezed together in bunk beds. Albert began to sense that something was not right.

'I remember my mum's face. When you live in a small house you realize when people don't get on. Mum would cook for the family, and then dad would cook for himself and he would sit downstairs.

'One day I came home and opened the front door. Dad was stood there and mum was stood there. Mum said, "Your dad's got to leave today because we got divorced". I couldn't even comprehend that, I was stunned.

'She said, "What do you want to do?" I couldn't think – I'm just seventeen. She says "I think you should go with your dad". So we left, left that house that day.'

It would be years before he would speak to his mother again.

For the next two nights, the aubergine Cortina was no longer a babe magnet. It was home.

It was hard because a serious accident had meant that Albert's father had to give up the haulage work. He began to operate as a taxi driver and they got themselves a bedsit in Moss Side. He recalls:

'We got this place in Moss Side – a bedsit. You've never seen such a hole. Rat droppings everywhere.'

The one thing they both had was a work ethic. Dad worked his taxis virtually every waking moment, whilst Albert studied and then taxied Thursday, Friday, Saturday and Sunday.

They were more savers than spenders. When they had accumulated some cash Albert suggested they get a house each. His father said they should get a better house between them. So, Albert went out and found a house in a good neighbourhood, he negotiated the price – £12,000, and set off to get a mortgage.

He laughs when he thinks about it.

'I walked in – I'm about 18 and there's a male and female. He's doing filing and she's busy doing something. I start talking: "I want to borrow some money." They just carried on doing what they were doing. They said "How much?" I said, "£8000, because I've got £4000 here".'

———————

Immediately they stopped what they were doing and started to pay attention. In those days £4000 was a lot of money. It taught Albert an important lesson. If you want to get something done, you have to get noticed, and so often money talks.

They got the house and he took responsibility for the décor. You can imagine what a boy with an aubergine Cortina would do to a house:

'I always wanted velvet flock wallpaper and I did the lounge myself.'
He collapses into hysterics as he remembers it.

'I did it and when it was done, I stepped back. You could see the lines of the paper were slightly off, there were white gaps between the sheets of flock.'

———————

Still, he made it home and could only then start to reconcile the hurt he felt when his mother had let him go. He says,

'When I think back, I think what my mother meant when she let me go was "Your father needs you".'

———————

Sharp knives and Sharp stereos

Stability reigned for a time, and Albert began a relationship. Albert's dad didn't like the fact that his girlfriend would stay at the house; he felt she may have something of a claim on it. Then Albert's dad told him he had a half-sister in addition to his other five sisters. She was having a few problems with her mother and was coming up from London to stay for a while.

'She was a lunatic, absolute lunatic. She didn't get on with my girlfriend. I bought a Sharp stereo system. It was the latest with graphics, the lot. I had an argument one day with her. I'd come home and the gas fires were on and I was paying the bills. Next thing I came home and the house is in darkness.

I noticed out of the corner of my eye something shining. She's coming at me with a butcher's knife. I left the house and she smashed my stereo to pieces.'

This caused a rift between Albert and his father about the ownership of the house. It ended up in court. Albert won and he never spoke to his father again.

Centres of influence

On finishing university, Albert hooked up with a friend who was brilliant at repairing TVs. He had the knowledge and Albert had the car, he laughs.

'I had the car, he was a great engineer – never made any bloody money but we did it.'

His first taste of business taught him that effort without results is pointless.

When he went to work for a small group which had filling stations and a car hire business, quite unconsciously, he began to apply the skills he had acquired tacitly at his mother's knee. The skills of observing people and situations and an ability to get on with people. People who could become centres of influence.

His sharp observational skills enabled him to notice how the staff were operating a 'fiddle'. They were pocketing the cash on the sale of oil, and simply topping up their display from an unlocked an uncontrolled storeroom.

His boss took on board his suggestions on how to tighten up procedures and put him in charge of three branches.

He could get on with people and he had some influential customers. One had noticed that Albert was bright and recommended him to NORWEB, the electricity board. He confided in Albert:

'A number of years ago I sat on an interview panel, and a black person came in, and I would have liked to appoint him, but the rest of the panel didn't want to. I don't think they will have met anyone like you. Ring this person and make an appointment.'

He got the job, studied part time at Manchester Business School, and began buying and renting properties to students, at first as a hobby, but it soon began to grow and grow. This young upstart middle manager now had the best car in the

NORWEB car park, and eyebrows were being raised. His easy way with people and his ability to spot and influence key variables began to irritate his immediate boss.

'I had to put together the financial statistics for the senior executives. There were four of them, all worried about my figures. They all had targets they had to achieve.

'I had a great relationship with them and they would invite me out to things. This undermined my boss. They always wanted to know how the figures were looking. Sometimes they'd panic and I'd say "I'll see what I can do". I realized I had a little bit of power. They used to invite me out socially. You can create a powerbase for yourself.

'One of them invited me out to a Christmas function. My boss rang him saying I had to come back. I didn't go back.' Typical Albert. 'This attitude would plague me for the rest of my life.'

It's true. Albert hates rules, authority or anyone trying to tell him what to do. His mother told him he was special, after all. When his boss conducted a disciplinary interview, he expected Albert to grovel. Instead he remembers that he didn't just dig his heels in, you would have thought that it was Albert doing the disciplining.

'I said: "Who do you think you are that you can speak to me like that?" His tash was twitching!'

Corporate life was not really for Albert, so he became an independent financial adviser whilst continuing to grow his property portfolio.

He had more freedom as a financial adviser and began to make big bonuses by looking for centres of influence that could make a difference, and by using his natural talents – an acute observational ability and a magical way with people. He thinks about the reasons for his success and says:

'What I could do was listen to rubbish and make business sense of it. Whilst some people had to see a lot of customers to meet their targets, I didn't. I did it with fewer visits because if you want to eat turkey, you don't hunt amongst the sparrows, do you? I had some big clients with high disposable income. I had their confidence. I had lawyers and doctors in my pocket, they were my friends, we studied together, socialized together.'

The property empire was growing too. He used the centres of influence he'd generated to great effect.

'All of my properties were let. Instead of just advertising like everybody else, I found out where the centres of influence were.'

He understood that universities had an accommodation officer. He made them his friends. It was no coincidence that his properties were always let.

Then rent officers started to become a nuisance.

'The rent officer could set the rent and he could reduce it. So I researched a case called Street vs. Mountford whereby a lawyer was letting property "on licence". The High Court ruled that it wasn't legitimate so everyone thought the licence was dead. Now hotels could let on licence, a non-exclusive licence. So, I'd show the whole house to tenants, all the rooms, and I'd issue them a non-exclusive licence. I introduced cleaners, they were my ears and eyes – and it was clean.'

To put more pressure on the centres of influence he helped form the Manchester Property Association, and bought a letting agents' business. He needed to make £22.50 a room whilst other landlords were charging £12–15. By having a stake in the agency, he was able to exercise a degree of control over rents, which, under his influence, began to creep up.

Then in 1990/91 interest rates escalated. Lots of people's property portfolios crashed. Albert's was one of them.

'I lost everything. It was like a pack of cards; everything crumbled. Everything was highly geared, it was a rising market and the bubble burst. Then I found out who my friends were.

'I said to a few close people that life was going to change. It changed me forever. I think I was on the verge of a nervous breakdown. A friend said, "Keep your costs low and tell no one anything". At one stage I couldn't raise a bean.'

Dark days and deals

When Albert took delivery of his Bentley Flying Spur, we were out for a drive,

84

Mike Cooper. More Overtaker than undertaker. Seen here completing his first London Marathon

Stewart and Jean Pickering, The Hippies, when they opened their first nursery which eventually became Kids Unlimited. Little did they know that the power of passion would create a business that turns over £30 million a year.

Selwyn Demmy, The Hustler, second from left with friends. From left to right, George Best who was at the time European Footballer of the Year, Selwyn, Alan Ball England's 1966 World Cup hero, and Gus Demmy, Selwyn's father.

Tim Bacon, The Soapstar, pays a visit to the Est Est Est restaurant in Alderley Edge, one of thirty four establishments owned by Living Ventures.

The author, pictured on the left with his hero in a photograph which he searched a lifetime for, and which only saw the light of day on the day that George Best was laid to rest.

Posh Spice. Karen Coleman, The Carer, takes a rare moment off work to 'Defy the Trade's Descriptions Act'.

Brad Friedel in his day job as the last line of defence for Blackburn Rovers making yet another save. The Times ranked him 14th out of 425 in their 2007 analysis of most valuable Premier League players.

Barely out of nappies in business terms, Bubbleboy Lee Mason, holding one of the 3,500 bottles of bubbly that he sells each year

Cottrill's jewellers in Wilmslow, one of the world's 100 most inspirational stores, dreamed up by The Alchemist, Karl Massey, over a couple of pints.

Always on the edge. Albert Edwards, The Prince, returns to the spot where he determined he would rebuild his life after losing everything.

Elaine James, The Magic Bean, with Shimba one of the three elephants she has adopted in Kenya's Tsavo National Park (copyright Elaine James)

Brad Friedel, The Rover, overseeing construction of his Premier Soccer Academy in Ohio.

and stopped for petrol. He filled up and got back in the car. He paused for a moment and just stared into space. I asked what he was doing and he gave an embarassed chuckle.

It was this very filling station he'd stopped at one day, in those dark days shortly after everything crashed. He sheepishly recounted the story.

'Things weren't working out, the money had gone. I would drive the kids to school. I thought I just about had enough petrol to get back. Then the car started juddering and I pulled in here. I went through my pockets I said to the kids, "Have you got any money, kids?" I searched down the back of the seats, and between us we had about 72 pence.

'The following day I went to my usual petrol station where they recognized me. I filled up with petrol – well they can't drain the tank can they? I said I'd forgotten my card, they said, "That's all right Albert; pay us next time".'

He had to earn a living, and he did all sorts of things – commodity broking; setting up a Caribbean dating agency; advising the Jamaican Post Office on modernization; dealing in second-hand prestige watches from big names such as Frank Mueller and Cartier.

Then a chance meeting on a plane opened up a new and totally unexpected centre of influence. Waiting for a plane in an airport departure lounge, Albert noticed an elderly, dapper gentleman who had an air of gentleness and elegance. Let's call him 'the Earl'. The Earl had noticed Albert's gold Frank Mueller watch. By sheer chance, they were seated together on the plane. They hit it off immediately and spent the next few hours opening up what was to become a remarkable influential friendship.

The Earl suggested that Albert get in touch and gave him his card. When Albert did his research on him he was stunned. This unassuming and charming fellow was a billionaire property owner and was building a conglomerate. Together they devised a way of buying companies in a tax-efficient way using offshore trusts, and Albert became one of the team that did the deals. The Earl began to refer people to Albert for advice.

This was the break he needed. The break which enabled him to get into his real passion – property – on a much bigger scale than before. Now he spends his time looking for sites with potential that others would steer clear of. His tenacious approach and attitude to risk means that he will battle harder and longer than normal property developers to get difficult or controversial planning permissions. It means that he will sit on properties longer than the commercial norm, because he has an extraordinary tolerance for risk.

When he wanted to get permission to build an extraordinary property on the same road as Sir Alex Ferguson, he put in a planning application for a 20,000 square foot house complete with a Sistine Chapel-style roof dome. There were fifty planning objections. One resident wrote to the local paper saying that it was a disgrace and it was like bringing the Trafford Centre (Manchester's massive retail shopping centre) to Cheshire.

Albert modified his plans to a 10,000 square foot house. The residents were delighted and it was passed. It was what he wanted in the first place, but he had realized that he would have to have a strategy for dealing with the influences – so he created a disaster scenario for them, and anything less was victory.

Today Albert has been able to swap his aubergine Cortina for a Bentley Flying Spur and a rat infested 'hole' for one of the Cheshire mansions he had always dreamed of.

His approach to everything is unorthodox, controversial, out of the box. It is the same when you ask him to give a tip for success. He says something totally unexpected. Something you will not find in any textbook, or on any business school course. He says, 'Listen to women'.

Growing up with five sisters and at his mother's knee has given him a remarkable ability which he uses to great effect. For many men, being caught up in women's company can be a difficult situation.

But to watch Albert in the company of women is quite remarkable. He seems to be on a different wavelength. He tunes in with them instantly and effortlessly, as if he's been made aware of some secret Masonic codeword.

He has found this to be remarkably useful in business, He says:

> 'Women have influenced my life. I've always been surrounded by them. I always surround myself with them. They give you information in a totally different way. They talk a lot, you have to decipher it. Women meet lots of people, they know all sorts of stuff and they want to talk about it. I listen to women because they know what's going on. You can find out about which houses are going to be sold even before they come on the market. Women have always encouraged me.
>
> 'I listen to gardeners and window cleaners as well. They know what's happening.'

His observational skills and his ability to tune into people give him the opportunity to uncover and exploit insights that others don't see. Modestly, he refers to himself as a 'general practitioner' in business, rather than a specialist. He has an eye for opportunity and has come a long way, but he will never forget those difficult days. He says:

'It's at those times that people inspire you. I always remember someone saying to me in my darkest hour, "Albert, surround yourself with people who make you smile, make you happy, feel positive. By doing that you'll have a good time; you won't feel down; you'll feel positive. If you surround yourself with negative people, it's like water on stone. Do you ever notice the slow drip? It leaves a mark, doesn't it – drip, drip, drip. A dirty mark.

'"You see all these negative people. They sit there and they talk about 'Well, I could have done this, and I would have been a millionaire.' They are losers. It's a way of authenticating their inability to make any impact on their lives".'

In Albert's dark days, a young man called Bob Marley, who became the god-father of reggae, looked down on the Jamaican bay where Albert's mother had played as a child. He wrote down some words:

Good friends we had
Good friends we lost
Along the way
In this great future you can't forget your past
So dry your tears I say

After coming through his dark days and finding out who his real friends were, Albert would no doubt concur with these words, and had he been there he would surely have asked Marley to add one more line to his song – 'Whatever happens you should never ever,ever,ever give up. Ever'.

Entrepreneurial insights from the Prince

- Create informal networks – Albert doesn't spend hours pouring over analyses, he creates enjoyable, informal settings where people share their information and knowledge.

- Look for insights in unusual places – for Albert, gardeners, window cleaners and, of course, women offer all sorts of insights and information.

- Be tenacious – building something up requires a tenacious attitude; so too does getting up off the floor when you have lost everything. There will be ups and there will be downs. Try to keep things in proportion if you encounter bad times. The worst thing that can happen is that you have to start again with a clean sheet of paper. Never ever, ever, ever, give up. Ever.

- Surround yourself with positive people. Business can be hard and precarious at times. You want people around you who will make positive suggestions, not try to make you feel more anxious than you already do. Positive people will make you laugh and smile and relax. A study published in the *Harvard Business Review* showed that the chemicals in the areas of the brain that govern creative thinking, become more active when you are relaxed.

8

The Hippies

'A negative can become a positive. It reminds you what you are about.'

There was no limo on that day in 1971 when Stewart and Jean Pickering tied the knot.

They arrived together at the church, with the roof down on their beat up, dark maroon Morris Minor convertible. The wind blew through golden blonde locks of hair – and that was just the groom.

Jean had made their wedding outfits herself. Matching multi-coloured embroidered kaftans recycled from old Indian bedspreads. They were hippies. They believed in love, passion, creativity, people, music, poetry, and togetherness. Marriage was their one gesture towards conformity. They didn't take too well to established ways of doing things.

Today, Kids Unlimited, a business set up by the Hippies, has a turnover of £30 million. Yet to them, this is nothing more than an incidental statistic in their story. **It was never about the money. It was about love, passion, creativity, people, music, poetry and togetherness. It was about breaking with the established way of doing things.**

A hippie business.

All you need is love

The Beatles had broken up a year earlier, yet the hippie movement continued into the seventies. It was a lifestyle, a counter-culture which embraced the values of anti-establishment, spirituality and sexual liberation. The hippies were heirs to the legacies of bohemians and beatniks.

For all that, Stewart was establishment by day, hippie in the evenings and at weekends. He had left university and taken a job with ICL, the computer giant, and in those days, computers themselves were giants. He says:

'I was commissioning big battleship mainframe computers, about the size of a pub, selling to the NHS and DHSS. Huge boxes with flashing lights.'

It was a respectable job, but he really felt most comfortable outside of the nine to five. He played guitar in a band, and that's how he came to the attention of a young fashion student called Jean. She remembers:

'Stewart was in a band as well as doing computers in the day. That was the thing that appealed to me about him, not his computer side. It was the more creative element that I saw. We just moved in together in Crumpsall with my friend. She was living with this musician guy.'

The four of them got on well, and Jean was offered a great job as a designer for Ladybird children's wear. It would have meant moving to London. Instead, all four of them loaded up a car with their meagre belongings and headed off in the opposite direction. They went to Kendal in the Lake District and lived in a commune.

They talk with great affection about those days. Jean says:

'A lot of the commune didn't have money. It was very idealistic. We'd all sit around at night talking Zen, doing yoga and playing guitars: it was a very beautiful situation. We made kaftans by hand from old Indian bedspreads.'

Whilst Stewart was bringing in his salary, other commune members would make leather belts and bags to sell on the markets, until eventually he gave up his job and they lived a life where material things just didn't seem to matter. What mattered were the relationships they had with other people, their freedom to create and their passion for what they were doing.

As with any institution or organization, no matter how informal, living in close proximity with other people has its challenges, and eventually these began to surface. Jean explains:

'You didn't have your own space. So when you got to know people's personalities it could actually become quite inhibiting. There was a conflict between those who wanted to be self-sufficient and work the markets, and those who just wanted to sign on and get their dole money.'

When Guru Maharaji came to England, some of the members of the commune joined his group. Stewart and Jean chose not to, and as the rifts began to deepen, they decided it was time to head back to Manchester.

The way things are stinks

There is a scene in the film *Babe* where Roseanna the duck is about to be eaten as Christmas dinner. Ferdinand the duck and one of the cows reflect on the situation where any one of them could end up in the same position. The cow is philosophical: 'The only way to find true happiness is to accept that the way things are is just the way things are.' Ferdinand begged to differ: 'The way things are *stinks!*'

Stewart and Jean tried to fit in. They tried to get on with 'the way things are'. Yet they found themselves more in tune with Ferdinand than the cow. Both became teachers, Stewart working in inner city schools and Jean, as she is apt to do, pursuing a more unconventional route, first working at a kind of Fame Academy and then at an experimental school in the middle of a park.

According to Stewart, these experiences were allowing them to understand what 'the system' was failing at and they began to unfold the principles upon which their business empire would be founded. Teaching was an eye-opener for both of them in different ways.

For Stewart, it was a case of fighting a losing battle. He says:

'It wasn't fighting a losing battle with the children. It was fighting a losing battle with the system. I think in many ways the children were actually nice kids; they were just in a setting which was oppressive. It was battling with the system more than with kids because the kids are kids. By the time they are fifteen or sixteen they have been completely conditioned to fail; then they haven't got a hope in hell.'

It was as if these children had missed out an important part of their development – play. All they seemed to want do was play; teaching was virtually impossible. Yet he liked the kids and they liked him. Other teachers frowned upon the fact that he allowed them to call him Stewart, yet in some ways he was getting through. At lunchtimes, pupils made a beeline for his classroom, where they could hang out, play guitars and listen to music.

He was having a hard time changing the system, but he was beginning to understand how these kids were thinking. He remembers one of his pupils in particular.

'She used to take orders for jumpers and things from Marks & Spencer's then she'd go out on a Saturday and steal to order and deliver to the kids. I said, "Surely that's wrong. Stealing is wrong". She said, "Yes, stealing is wrong but nicking is alright". I said, "What's the difference?" She said, "Well, if you get caught, it's stealing. If you don't, it's nicking". I was fighting a losing battle.'

At least he had his music. He was in band called Pegasus and this was his passion. The big record deal was always just around the corner so Stewart took on a couple of rooms next to a church where they could practise. His talent for engineering saw it evolve into a recording studio which they called Graveyard Sounds. Jean can take up this bit of the story later.

In the meantime, she was undergoing her own enlightenment in a school opposite Manchester's Strangeways prison. She says:

'I got a job in a place called the High School of Art. I was very lucky because I'd done all these creative subjects and when I came out the Head of Department was on a secondment. So in my first probationary year I got Head of Department of Dance. It was a school that was a wreck, but the creativity that went on there was just unbelievable. So I had to do all these dance shows and exhibitions, I was just thrown in.'

It had the same kind of creative buzz as the school portrayed in the musical *Fame*, and Jean loved it, but when the Head of Department returned she was out of a job. She found work in an extraordinary experimental school in the centre of Manchester's Heaton Park. Three groups of children would come from three different schools and stay for three weeks. She says:

'You would mix them together and you would get the Moss Side kids flinging the Jewish wide-brimmed hats around like frisbees. You would have to let it just shake down and then try to work with them in a creative way. This is where my thing for working with young children started'.

The kids would be encouraged to think about things in all sorts of creative ways using dance, poetry, art and expression. Jean's approach was to get the kids started by doing something that they could be successful at and then working up from there. This, and listening to Stewart's stories of kids being set up to fail, began to colour her philosophy.

'I used to have these seven-year-olds saying "I can't, I can't". I thought, where have these words come from that tells children of this age they are failures? That they are rubbish at this and rubbish at that? You can actually talk to children in a way that encourages success.'

She noticed how negative the visiting teachers could be, often saying that you could work creatively in the experimental setting, but not back in the school setting. She strongly disagreed and the seed of an idea was sown. She says:

'This is why I felt that it was so important to get to them before they got into the school system, and that was where the whole early years thing came in for me. But we weren't able to take this on yet because we had another journey to take first.'

The other journey was Graveyard Sounds, Stewart's recording studio which was beginning to get something of a name for itself. He began to get some paid work as a recording engineer and things began to snowball. Anthony Wilson, whose time setting up Factory Records and The Hacienda nightclub is depicted in the film *Twenty Four Hour Party People*, began to use Graveyard Sounds. The band Joy Division was big at the time and recorded at Graveyard. They were all in the studio shortly after they heard that lead singer Ian Curtis had committed suicide, with Anthony Wilson trying to deal with the aftermath and handling press calls.

Jean, who had now had her first child Simon, recalls happier Graveyard moments.

'Then we had a fantastic band in called Sad Café. They were just amazing. What we had was this studio that was suddenly becoming commercial. There was one day I came downstairs with Simon and they were having smoked salmon and champagne, it was so exciting – they had been given a big advance.'

Later they were to chart at number three with their single *Everyday Hurts*.

This minor success led to a merger with Revolution Studios on the south side of Manchester, and Jean began to become frustrated. Firstly, this was a passion for Stewart, but she couldn't get passionate about something that seemed to consume more and more of their money. In addition, Stewart was working the night shift at the studios and she was stuck at home with a young child.

She started to look for a nursery for Simon and just didn't like what she was seeing.

> 'You either had a Social Services nursery that wasn't creative or you had the prep schools. I put Simon into one of these prep schools and he was coming home with exercise books at the age of two, to be marked. His work was being marked, "Good boy", it said. He hadn't done anything. Somebody had drawn something and he was expected to do something within it. I wanted him to do his own stuff so I was very frustrated with that.'

Then one night Stewart came home from the studio with the news that Jean didn't want to hear. The studio needed more investment and another trip to see the bank manager was needed. Jean is animated about that even today.

> 'I just said forget it. We are not putting any more money into this. I am setting up a nursery because I can't go back to work, because I can't find suitable childcare for Simon. There may not be suitable childcare for him, but I believe that there can be and I am going to do it.'

Red shoes for the Reeves girl

They sold their house and rented until they could find suitable premises for a nursery. For two years they kept coming up against problems with Planning Officers who appeared to want to create 'nursery-free zones'. Then a phone call came out of the blue and Jean remembers she was lying on the sofa feeling ill as she took the call:

> 'I got this call from a lady who owned Claremont Nursery saying, "I've got this playgroup and I want to sell it". We went to see it, because I had driven past it. I have a habit of driving past places, it's as if I've put my mark on it and it comes back round to me.
> 'I was very intuitive. If you do things with this open heart, are genuine

and you are not trying to rip someone off, then these things often do come to you.'

Somehow, quite naturally their talents have seemed to complement each other. Jean had the vision and drive and Stewart could be single-minded and good with figures. He was able to make business sense of Jean's instincts and passions, though he laughs now when he thinks about that first business plan in 1983.

'It was so basic. The percentages were crazy. We had £5000 and we wanted to borrow £60,000, yet we delivered the presentation to the Co-op Bank with such passion that they believed in us.'

They drew on their teaching experiences, the good and the bad, and set out to create a kind of nursery that was different. Not for the sake of being different, but because they passionately believed that what they were doing was the right thing. Jean explains the philosophy:

'It was very much about creating the environment and the repertoire, the equipment and the skills of the teachers to *facilitate* the learning, rather than dictating the learning. At the ages of two, three and four, children need to experiment, to try things out, they need to make mistakes, but they don't need to see those mistakes as failures.'

In the eighties, such ideas were unprecedented and Jean found that that there was a big job to be done in educating the parents. She says:

'The kids would come out with these drawings that weren't the mass-produced drawings they were getting from other nurseries, the kind of thing where the member of staff will draw a cat. Why can't the child draw their own cat?

'Our children would bring their work out and the parents would say, "What's that?" I would say, "Please don't say to a child that has produced this work of art, 'What's that?' Just say, 'Tell me about it'," and then the child would say, 'There's the tail; there's the head', and then you can start to see it. Sometimes scribbles are the most important things that children do at that age.

'We had to engage the parents, and the parents had to engage with us, because we weren't there to just take money. That wasn't what it was all about. For me the passion was to have parents being excited by their children's endeavours to create. That was what it was all about.'

Jean knew she was doing something different. She wanted to establish aesthetic buildings and creative environments. That first nursery was converted in just six weeks. As they worked through the night to get it finished, the last thing they did was to paint the floor bright red. The effect was stunning, but Jean was distraught when one of football's first million pound men Kevin Reeves came to collect his daughter Bianca. The paint on the floor was barely dry and her beautiful shoes had turned bright red. It didn't matter – the atmosphere was so lively and vibrant that many of the parents became long-standing friends.

Growing pains

Parents were beginning to get the idea. Whereas other nurseries were trying to convince parents that their children should be reading and writing at two years old, Jean was preaching a gospel of creativity, play and fun. When she introduced all-day care some parents were sceptical, believing that their children wouldn't stay for lunch, but Jean was ahead of her time again.

'The food was all fantastic. This was 26 years ago. Never mind Jamie Oliver; we were doing totally additive-free food with no colourings or preservatives. If you believe in something and talk about it in truth and honesty then people can't argue with that. I believed that it was the right thing for these children.'

Word spread rapidly, and they continued to innovate by taking in babies. In less than twelve months the place was absolutely full. They lived in an attic room above the nursery, and with a young child of their own things were cramped, to say the least. Jean was beginning to think she could set up another nursery, but was worried about losing control.

When the bungalow next door came up for sale Jean felt that they should buy it, but Stewart was concerned about not having planning permission. Jean was adamant that they were going to get planning permission and after Stewart went away and did the sums again, they agreed to buy it.

When the planning application went in, the local councillor sided with residents who were objecting. Jean argued her case on the roadside; the planners and residents on one side, her on the other. They were not going to give up. Stewart did a survey of where people travelled in from and at what times, showing that, unlike a school, the drop-off and pick-up times were staggered. They lobbied other local councillors, because demand for nursery places was outstripping supply. Finally, they went to the planning meeting and provided every councillor, except their local one, with a dossier of their findings. They had taken a leap of faith in buying this property. Everything hinged on the outcome of this meeting. Jean remembers it well.

'The local councillor was so negative. He stood up and just thought he had it nailed. He moved a motion to reject the application.

'Then the pages started to turn, people were looking through this document we had given them. He was totally freaked out, and when they went to the vote everybody supported us except him. He was devastated.'

Spiritual partner

Jean was besotted by this business, and Stewart managed to slow her down from time to time. On a trip to Haworth in Yorkshire, Jean visited a spiritualist who told her, 'You will have a little Rose'. It was Stewart's persuasion rather than spiritual guidance that convinced Jean to have a second child. The little rose was named Sadie, and according to Stewart it is something more than a mother-daughter relationship. He says:

'They are really spiritual partners. Sadie has inherited Jean's talent for drama and dance and is living out the life that Jean would have loved. Theirs is a special and unique closeness.'

Sadie was doing professional acting work from the age of ten, including parts in *Children's Ward*, *24/7*, *At Home with the Braithwaites* and *Heartbeat*, amongst others.

So with two children of their own to juggle, the chance to innovate again came soon after. The Refuge Assurance Company was relocating to Wilmslow and there were not enough nursery places for their staff. Jean and Stewart suggested that they run a workplace nursery, something commonplace today, but at the time unheard of. They were going to have to tender for it, and again this was another new experience. Their tender documents may not have been as strong as others, but their secret weapon paid off yet again – passion. They believed in what they were doing. They wanted it and they got it.

Time bomb

Sometimes you just get yourself into the right place at the right time. When the Midland Bank published a report about the implications of an impending demographic time-bomb, Kids Unlimited, as they now called themselves, found they were in a perfect position.

According to the report, Britain would need thousands of new nursery places if women were to be able to return to work. The media got hold of the childcare agenda in a big way. Kids Unlimited had the mix of private and workplace nurseries; they became the people to talk to and Jean's obvious passion for what she was doing shone through. She was featured in TV series *Women Today* with Anita Roddick; they were in the *Guardian* and *The Daily Telegraph*. They were beginning to realize that a big opportunity was opening up.

Soon they were running workplace nurseries for the Midland Bank, the Body Shop and the NHS. The beauty of it was that they were building a business using other people's capital assets. Their job was to apply their formula and their passion. At the same time, their own assets were appreciating in value. They found themselves in a great position at the forefront of this new workplace nursery movement.

It's interesting how they thought about growth. They didn't devise a complex strategic plan, they just thought to themselves, 'Who will get as passionate as we are about this?' Jean simply picked up the phone. First she tried to get Richard Branson at Virgin.

'I thought, "He will believe it", but I couldn't get through to him. But I got through to the Body Shop and they said, "Ah we are talking to a company at the moment". I said, "Well, you shouldn't be talking to anybody but us". This is what I was like on the phone. I'm thinking is this really me? But I believed that we had to do the Body Shop nursery – not for money, but because there was an empathy and we needed to work with people like that. That was the buzz for me, getting that contract, working with people who are like-minded.'

Being committed to the quality of their operations, Stewart applied for a grant to set up a training programme, and got it – £100,000 which was about 20% of their turnover at the time. They felt that investing heavily in staff was the right thing to do and it would help them to keep good people. Jean thought it was absurd that an eighteen-year-old could come out of college with a qualification and get paid more than a woman returner who had brought up her own children. So they preferred to employ women who wanted to come back to work and develop them whilst they were on-the-job and getting paid. Two years later the government introduced National Vocational Qualifications (NVQs) that worked exactly in this way and the Kids Unlimited programme required only minor tweaking to become an accredited NVQ. Once again, they were ahead of their time. Not because they were trying to be, simply because they were driven by their passion and their belief in doing the right thing.

Things were taking off and when they were offered outside investment through a Business Expansion Scheme (BES), they took it. The idea of BES was that it allowed investors to avoid tax if they injected cash and expertise into a business with good growth potential.

Stewart and Jean at first welcomed the new investors. But it was the beginning of a nightmare which saw them almost losing Kids Unlimited. Jean says:

'The idea of a BES is that investors take a back seat. The nature of their personalities wouldn't allow them to take a back seat.

'On Friday afternoons they would go through every cheque that was going out. They targeted Stewart in a board meeting about a milk bill that was next to nothing. Stewart is the most honest person ever – I would try and manipulate stuff, but he is honest to a fault and this little milk bill had slipped through, and they just destroyed him in this meeting. He's being philosophical and I'm thinking never again. We never lose control of the company.'

They were on the brink of losing control and when they found out that the investors had been negotiating with a competitor to take control of Kids Unlimited, a meeting was called at the company solicitors. For Jean, this was one of those 'bang the table' moments.

'We were all sitting around this table and I knew they all had these large houses and loads of money and this was our little company that we had allowed them to come into. I said "This is our company, this is my life, I have a child to look after and how can you possibly justify doing this to us?" I banged the table and said how can you go home at night and sleep, knowing that we are totally honest people who have worked so bloody hard for this. You are taking a company from us leaving us with nothing.'

Passion won the day again. The investors agreed to take a pay-off for their investment. So Stewart took a loan from his parents, both swallowed hard and paid off the investors for a loss.

They had had a harsh lesson in business from some tough cookies. They found it hard to believe that someone could try to take their business away from them like that. So for the next seven years they stepped out of the limelight and decided to concentrate upon what they were really good at – running nurseries. They grew steadily and organically.

That is, until Jean had another one of her visions. She had the idea of creating something that was of a scale, but had all the features of the special environment that Kids Unlimited was known for. She went out to look at nurseries in Italy, Scandinavia, Germany, Holland and the USA. She liked some of the ideas she had seen in Italy and had an architect design something that could accommodate 100+ children and yet feel like a small nursery in a big nursery. Children would be based in small 'home units' and have piazza areas where they could meet and play.

A project on this scale needed substantial investment, so again they took investment capital. The targets that the investors set began to erode the concept. According to Jean:

> 'When we took on investors, we were targeted to fill those open spaces and that's where it became compromised. For me as a parent it's nice that you go in you feel space, you don't feel kids all around.
>
> 'One set of investors wanted us to fill, fill, fill, which was counterproductive. You may get more people in, but you get people in because of the concept that you created in the first place, which was space. So as you fill the space, it becomes unattractive – you have lost the concept. It's better to keep it small, intimate, spacious; and then ramp up your fee.'

New investors have taken the business further, and Stewart and Jean now take a back seat. A full-time management team looks after the day-to-day running of the business, which now has 46 nurseries, and a turnover of £30 million.

It was built on passion. It was never really about the money. Passionate people have to have an outlet, and Stewart and Jean are struggling with this. They still part-own their business, but have little part to play in it. For the moment they are lost. They know that there is another chapter to come in their lives; yet their state of limbo, neither being out of the business nor in it, is preventing them from turning the page.

Stewart reflects on all that has happened. 'Here's a message to any other entrepreneurs. If you are going to exit the business, sell it in one lot.' He likens their experience to the choice that you have when you remove a sticking plaster. You can pull at it a bit at a time and prolong the pain or get it over with and pull it off in one go. He feels they should have broken their connection with the business in one go.

They didn't, and it has brought a lot of frustration and heartache. He says:

'Now we still have shares – no control and no job, but we are OK financially. The message here is if you are going to stay in a business, do not lose control, otherwise it feels like you are pulling at an Elastoplast. The pain is prolonged.'

For the moment, Stewart has invested in Revolution Studios and you can see that music is a passion of his. There are three elements to the business. The studio, which he readily admits will never make a fortune. Secondly, their own record label which has just released its first single, *Palisades* by Puressence; and they have signed up Jimmy Catto, formerly with Faithless. Then there is the sound library, which according to Stewart is *the* big thing. He says:

'It's a product for the music industry. If somebody is recording at home, what they can't do is create a drum sound, which requires an ambience. We have a deal with an American company which will go worldwide.

'They can buy a CD with, say, 900 different variations. It's ahead of the field in terms of quality and flexibility. For example, we have recorded snare drum patterns; not single hits. Drum machines are hits. In this library, the fill is played, we have six mikes on the snare drum so you can create a very close sound. When you put it back together you can't tell this is not from a real drum.

'A guy who knows drummers, Andy, was playing this back and he said, "That's Paul Burgess – 10CC's drummer", and it was. Although it's recorded separately, in bits, it's got the same feeling. It's awesome. So that's a music product and the rest of the business …'

As Stewart enthuses about the music business, he looks over at Jean's eyes. He knows it is time to stop enthusing.

There is something missing from the eyes of the Hippie girl.

It is passion.

The music business just doesn't do it for her and together they wonder how they will find the passion that they once felt for Kids Unlimited. They have a place in Deia in Majorca, and they think that maybe they will turn it into a creative sanctuary for musicians.

Maybe they will. But not until Jean's eyes sparkle with passion again.

Entrepreneurial insights from the Hippies

- Look for things that you are dissatisfied with. Entrepreneurs often create new products and services by trying to fix something that doesn't work too well. Jean felt that the available childcare provision just didn't offer what she was looking for, whilst Stewart's experiences suggested that children were missing out an important stage of their development – play. If you are dissatisfied with something, chances are, other people will be too. If you can find a way to bridge the gap, you might have the embryo of a new business.

- Have something at stake. When you put your own money and lifestyle on the line, failure is not an option. Stewart and Jean sold their house, invested £5000 and borrowed £60,000. They could not afford to fail. They have an attitude that says, whatever the problem, they will always find a route around it.

- Passion can move mountains. Make sure that whatever you are doing excites you, drives you, makes you want to jump out of bed in the morning. Stewart and Jean would not usually have been funded so highly as a start-up were it not for the passion and conviction they showed; they may have lost their planning battle on the second nursery were it not for passion; they should never have won their first workplace nursery tender, yet passion won through. It has been the driving force in their business and their lives. You cannot learn it at any business school. If you want to rediscover your passions see my other book, *Bear Hunt – Earn your living by doing what you love*, Chapter Two.

- If you are going to stay in a business, never lose control of the running of it. If you are going to exit, it can be best to do it cleanly and in one go. Check and research your options thoroughly and be clear about how much involvement you want to retain.

9

The Maverick

'Life. It's the best thing that ever happened to me.'

It was a hot summer. Corporate HQ was awash with men in smart short-sleeved shirts and stay-pressed trousers. Unusually, there was a buzz about the corporate canteen.

The buzz concerned a young whippersnapper project manager Andy White. In his naivety, he had taken on the job that everyone had refused: to construct a new grandstand at Manchester City's Maine Road in time for the new season. He had just fourteen weeks. As if that wasn't enough, he had promised to quit if he failed to do it. He would be the scapegoat for the men in suits.

If he succeeded the company would bank £1 million for just fourteen weeks' work. For every day that the project exceeded the fourteen weeks, the company would be penalized by £50,000. A small slip-up and a profit could become a loss as well as a high-profile humiliation for the company. No wonder this job was being tossed around like a hot potato.

Word was getting around. The kid was delivering the goods. Not only was he going to come in on time, he was going to finish a week early. There was glory to be had, and the men in corporate HQ wanted a piece of it.

One by one, they began to turn up on site and bask in the reflected glory. Andy White could feel the steam coming out of his ears. As yet another senior executive pulled up in the car park, he was waiting for him. By now he was furious. One leg of a pair of stay-pressed trousers made its way out of the car. Before the other leg could follow, Andy slammed the door against corporate man and made his position clear.

'Get back in the car. I don't want you on this site. You've never been to see me for fourteen weeks, you ain't coming now. Piss off.'

For the maverick, this was to be the moment. The moment when he began to think he could do this for himself, and, perhaps, it was time he did.

Since then, he has been successful as an entrepreneur and then lost everything; he has brought his maverick style to bear on a business within a plc, turning it around from being the worst performer to the best in just three years; and now, back in business as an entrepreneur, he went from nothing to £175 million in little more than nine months.

Not bad for a man who says he is not particularly good at anything. Nothing, that is, except for having an innate ability to get on with people.

The man who stopped work only for a pope

Andy White is a driven man, yet his style is not to ride roughshod over people; he has been successful because of an amazing ability to get people on his side. He is the kind of guy that you would like to have on your side. If people are willing to fight for the cause, whatever it may be, he will coax, cajole, mentor, coerce, develop, support – whatever it takes to win. If people don't get behind the cause he is not afraid to bruise a few egos – if you are disengaged and wearing stay-pressed trousers, you may end up with a bruise to more than just your ego.

There is no hiding place on a building site, and that's where he began to hone his people skills. He arrived as a young graduate, a fresh-faced General Foreman, and was immediately brought down to earth. He says:

'The humour brings you down to earth very quickly. One of the first lads I ever met was called Pat Leahy.'

Pat was a hardened Irish builder with a mischievous twinkle in his eye. His first words on meeting Andy were, 'Jesus, Andrew. Oi believe you've just left school.' Andy responded politely, 'I have Pat, yes.' Pat looked him up and down. 'How old are you, Andrew?' Still smiling, Andy replied that he was twenty-two. Pat tilted his head and twinkled his eyes as he reflected on this. 'Well, you do look a bit slower than the rest of us. We all left school at fourteen.'

Andy enjoyed this little exchange as much as Pat, even though the joke was on him. He has a natural way with people which is central to his overall philosophy in business and in life. He says:

'I'm not very good at anything, but the biggest attribute, if I've got any-thing at all, is people skills. Because if you manage, coax, coerce, and men-tor people you can do anything. Get people on your side and you can do anything, anything at all. It doesn't matter what it is. Treat everybody with respect. Respect all, fear no one.'

His drive to get things done and his ability to get people to follow him saw Andy rapidly rise up the ranks of Laing's construction business and he was soon number two on a major hospital construction. Then the boss called him in. He told Andy that he was looking for someone to manage the new grandstand at Manchester City, saying that it was a £1 million job, to be done in fourteen weeks with a penalty clause of £50,000 a day. He asked Andy, 'Do you think you can do it?' Without hesitation he replied, 'Yes'.

Somewhat taken aback the boss said, 'You haven't seen it'. Andy remembers his response.

'I said, "I'll do it". The boss looks at me and says "If you don't do it, will you Jack?" [Meaning, "Will you resign?"] I said "Is that what you want me to do? OK, I'll agree to that", and I shook his hand.'

It was a demanding job.

'It had thrills, spills, strikes and health and safety issues. I realized he must have asked a few people before me who had said no. I thought, I've got a career ahead of me, I'm not bothered, I will do it. That's naivety really, but I just thought to myself, whatever it takes, I will do it. And we did.'

He was a tenacious maverick with a real gift for getting people to get things done. He lived and breathed the job. It would have taken a pope to stop him. In fact it did. In the whole fourteen weeks he took half a day off to ensure that his wife could go to see Pope John Paul II on his visit to Manchester.

He was doing well, but he began to feel the beginnings of an unscratchable itch.

No thicko

He admits to this itch he just can't scratch. Every morning he wakes up wanting to go out and prove himself again. Even now, he says, 'I wake up in the morning and think I'm skint.' It is what gets him out of bed.

It is a feeling that he has always had and he feels he can trace it back to an event in Primary School. Something that caused him to feel separate, different. He recalls how his teacher asked his mother to come into the school.

> 'They said to my mother, "Your son is a long, long way behind the other children. He will need extra lessons, extra reading at home. Have you any books at home? No. Well, I think you ought to get these books". When I heard those words I thought that will never ever happen to me again in my life.'

_____

This incident had a dramatic effect and created in Andy some kind of intense drive because over the next four years his progress was remarkable:

> 'I moved up from being bottom of the bottom stream to the top three in the top stream. I passed for Bolton and Manchester Grammar Schools but failed the interviews and ended up at Stand Grammar School.'

_____

Subsequently, he went on to university, which may sound quite normal now, but if you were from the tough Salford neighbourhood that Andy grew up in, it was a feat little short of flying to the moon.

He would not allow himself to be branded what he terms a 'thicko'. Yet it happened again, this time at the age of twenty-seven. Perhaps it reignited that insatiable drive.

He remembers how it happened.

> 'I had £300 in the bank. I've got a baby, Natalie, who was two. My missus was just about to have our second child in five weeks' time. I went home one night and said, "I've had it with that. I'm having a go on my own". It went down like a lead balloon, especially with my in-laws. They couldn't believe it. They came round and said, "Are you stupid? You've got a wife, two babies, a mortgage, and no money". I said "I'll make it work".'

_____

He had no clear idea of what he was going to do to make it work, just an un-shakable belief in his own ability to make things happen. He risked everything. The £300 in the bank was probably enough to cover his day-to-day living costs for about a month. Everything was in the balance. He had no choice but to make something work. Now he had an added incentive. After all he had been through, someone had had the audacity to suggest he was stupid. The Maverick rolled up his sleeves.

So where did he start? He didn't start with a business plan that's for sure. His brother was in the business of building house extensions and had got wind of somebody who wanted an office block building. Andy's first job was to get the contract for the construction of that office block. Sure, he knew quite a lot about construction, but he had absolutely no track record in business. He went to Blackburn to see the man concerned, and all he could do was let his natural ability to get on with people kick in. He came back with the contract for the office block. It was, he remembers, £305,000. Once he had a foot in the door he was determined to impress. And he did.

> 'From that we built every phase on that site for the next four years. Using that as a base we expanded into doing our own residential developments, flats, nursing homes. We built the business on the back of that first contract.'

He even built a nursery for a couple of Hippies. Stewart and Jean Pickering who you heard about in Chapter Eight remember him well. At Christmas he brought presents for all the children.

Perhaps he was not so stupid after all. He was the man without a plan. The Maverick with a talent for getting things done and taking people with him. After fourteen years of growth, he was riding high.

The late 1980s was a tough time for everyone in the construction industry, yet he got through it. Then came the 1990s, and with it an interest rate spiral to a level nobody could have predicted. Andy reflects on this.

> 'The early nineties, with the advent of interest rates of between 15 and 17 per cent and moving very quickly, spelt disaster. When you have done your numbers on 8%, you are in trouble. In 1994 we lost everything we had. We lost the lot. Yes, the lot.'

Having had an exemplary record with the bank, he imagined that they would be supportive and see him through the crisis.

> 'The bank was supporting us throughout all our developments. The construction company was very successful, but the construction company was guaranteeing all the interest payments for the development side. We had

always had an overdraft facility on the construction side of £500,000 and never touched a penny of it in ten years. The minute we started to touch it, the bank removed it; and we had personal guarantees to cover that, shares, houses. The minute we started to touch it the bank pulled it away. It all happened very quickly after that. I lost my personal assets. Paid the loans and guarantees off over a period of time.'

As if losing everything wasn't enough, he was going through a protracted divorce at the same time. Some people would have been destroyed by this. For Andy White it became a spur. Perhaps it brought back that same feeling he had when his teachers told him he wasn't coming up to scratch. He remembers how it felt in those difficult days.

'There were times when you would wake up in the morning and think "Well, there is no way today is going to be as bad as yesterday", and it turns out to be worse. So you experience that, but that kick in the teeth gives you a spur to go and do other things.'

Without trying, perhaps without even noticing, he had built up a reputation in the industry. He had got himself noticed. One of those who had noticed him was the Chairman of the construction giant, Sir Alfred McAlpine. They had a problem with one of their businesses and the Chairman rang Andy to see if he would consider coming to work for them to sort it out.
For the Maverick, this represented a dilemma.

'I thought that's not me – going back to working for somebody else. The Chairman said, "We will make it worth your while", I thought, "Well, what have I got to lose? I haven't got any money".'

So the corporate world of stay-pressed trousers and short-sleeved shirts beckoned.

A Maverick in a corporate world

Inevitably there were some culture clashes. Andy's approach was entrepreneurial. He was quick on his feet, hands-on and had little time for paper shuffling. He had to adapt to his new surroundings, but he knew if anything spectacular was going to happen he would have to get his people to adopt a different way of working and to pull together as a team.

He describes how he started to motivate the people. At an early briefing of the senior managers, Andy put his cards on the table.

'Listen. The company's got a problem. Here's where we are. Here's where we are going and here's the route we are going down to get there.'

One of the managers, an engineer with a first class honours degree, couldn't contain his scepticism. He stood up in the meeting and in front of the whole senior management team addressed Andy directly:

'The jury is out on you. I've never heard so much bullshit in my life.'

Andy remained unflustered, but was intrigued. He says:

'He was an aggravating bastard. He and I became closer over time, because he had to have some bottle to do that in a room full of senior people. As I got to know him better, I said, "Michael, what do you want out of your life? What are your goals in life, what are your aims?" He said, "I don't know – I've never really thought about it".'

Andy suggested that he go away and brainstorm what his goals might be, and to come back so that together they could prioritize them and put timescales to them, which he did. This was not some clever tactical ploy on the part of Andy White; it was born out of a genuine desire to help someone. In the process, it turned a sceptical enemy into a positive ally. It also acted as an eye-opener for Andy. He had noticed something that had never occurred to him before. 'I think the majority of people in the world are like that. They've never had any goals.' He had to set some goals and get people to believe in them rather quickly – he had uncovered bad news, the company was in dire straits.

He blames it on the culture of the organization. It had been a family firm which floated on the stock exchange. An influx of investment and new people had created complacency and a business that was slow to react to changes in the marketplace. Procedures and controls were lax and the company was sitting on serious annual losses with a negative cash position. Something had to change.

As if this wasn't enough, he found that the employees were living in some kind of corporate cloud cuckoo land. The shiny corporate offices, chauffeur-driven cars and even company airline pilots had everybody believing they were doing well, even though the balance sheet suggested otherwise.

Mavericks don't mess about. Just as he had built a grandstand against the odds in less than fourteen weeks, by deciding what had to be done and sticking at it doggedly, he set about stemming the losses and turning the company around. He made more than 500 people redundant, a difficult decision when some people had been with the firm 35 years; changed the structures, procedures and controls; tightened up cash management; and overhauled risk assessment and management. Most importantly, he began to work on the people to change the culture of the organization, changing the thinking, the belief systems, and gradually getting corporate stalwarts to face up to reality and place their feet on terra firma.

They didn't know how to take him. He was totally unorthodox, yet they had to put up with him because he was delivering the goods. Having gone in to sort out an ailing part of the business, he became a roving trouble-shooter and was then put in charge of the whole construction business.

Nobody knew what to expect. What was the Maverick going to do next? He worked relentlessly on creating a culture which kept people's feet on the ground. His board meetings were a case in point.

'Every third quarter board meeting I used to go in the night before with flip charts, write messages on them and pin them up around the walls.'
Things like:
- 'Don't believe in your own bullshit'
- 'Who do you think you are?'
- 'The cleaner is the most important person in this company.'
- 'Think about the fact that within twelve months we may not have in existence a single client that you know today.'
- 'Where is your new business coming from?'
- 'How much is a gallon of petrol? If you don't know give me your credit card.'
- 'When was the last time you said thank you to your staff?'
- 'When was the last time you praised your staff?'
- 'In your department who is causing you the biggest threat? Tell me who it is. I'll train them and develop them until they are no longer a threat.'

This was not the paper shuffling buzzword bingo that these corporate types were used to and it caused more than a little consternation. He laughs.

'They used to go absolutely mad. They detested it. "Why are you doing all of this?" they would ask.'

When he delivers his response to the question, the passion is evident even today. He says 'it's to keep us all on our toes.'

Though he is proud of his success in the corporate world he describes it more as 'survival' in a setting where he was never totally comfortable. He had his own way of doing things.

'I used to procure opportunities in pubs, bars, wine bars, wherever I thought there was opportunity, that's where I would go. Whatever I had to do to get opportunity, that's what I did. They would say, 'How did you get that opportunity, why has nobody else got it, why didn't we get those opportunities before you came? We don't understand this – nothing seems to have changed, but everything's changed. Why's that?'

Things changed because as well as working with the people, he was hungry, fleet of foot, intuitive and he wasn't afraid to take risks. He has a beer mat in his office which he is very proud of. It is a reminder of how he was able to take an entrepreneurial approach into a corporate setting. He remembers meeting a friend for a drink in London's Berkeley Square.

'I've still got the beer mat. A lad I used to see for a drink said to me, "My pal has got an opportunity. It's a shopping centre. Will you meet him?" He drew this shopping centre on a beer mat, told me what the income was, drew the site around it. I said, "Right, based on that here's our offer." He said "I'll recommend that to him for approval." That's now done, dusted, built, occupied and sold again. That was on the back of a beermat. Well, two sides. One was his drawing, the other was my offer.

'I still think they are the best deals to do. Admittedly there has to be a lot of legal work.

'There will always be loads of guys around saying you've got it wrong and doubting you because it's not been through a process where 27 people have signed up to it. When you start to have a few successes like that then people begin to believe in you.'

He has had many successes like that, and he firmly believes in celebrating success. For the men in stay-pressed trousers, he remained an enigma.

'Sometimes on a Friday I would go to work in shirt, shorts and flip flops. On a Friday afternoon I would open my doors and say come and give me your request for what you want on the music box. If I didn't have it, if they

111

gave me a week's notice, I would try to get it. I used to play it top blast. So we had a bit of a party atmosphere at times. Celebrate success, but when you are in the shit you all pull together. A bit like the army I suppose.'

But corporate types are corporate types and they like structure and order. When a colleague from the Human Resources Department came to see Andy, he presented him with a huge manual and asked him to read it over the weekend. It was called the Genesis Project and it was to be the company's new way of managing people. Andy chuckled. He had been successful using his own system of management, and didn't need a manual – he could write it down on a beer mat. He says:

'We had our own way of doing HR which was straight, honest and open at all times. People were the most important thing in the world, and you should ensure you are always straight with them. Be as strong as an oak and bend like a willow.'

Some weeks later he and the Human Resources colleague were standing in a queue at a hotel reception.

'It was interesting. It was raining, thundering and lightning outside. There was a long queue and the girl behind reception was trying her best, but she was clearly flustered, so I'm waiting patiently. He goes up and bangs the bell and says, "Do you know who I am? When will my room be ready?" I pulled him to one side and said "Hey. You know that manual you gave me? Is that what it says in the chapter on how to handle people?"'

The Wacky Warehouse way to wealth

For a square peg in a round hole he did an extraordinary job. He was offered the post of CEO, but couldn't see himself continuing in a corporate setting. He took a holiday and whilst he was in the pool with his son Sam, he asked him what had been the best thing about their week away. The response he got was to seal his decision about his future. Sam looked up and said, 'The best thing about this holiday has been seeing my daddy every day.' Andy says:

'That was what made me change. I thought right, well, I'll go and do something different.'

So once again he did. He left the corporate world not knowing what he was going to do; just that it was time to start out again. He began to look around.

'I just started to look around at opportunities as diverse as I could find. Anything. Anything at all. Particularly where there was a problem that needed to be solved. Or where there may be an opportunity from solving a problem. I thought I'll go and do something that nobody else wants to touch. The chances are that somewhere there will be money there. At the time I looked at hotels, factories, brownfield sites, pits that had closed down, automotive after care sales, all types of business.'

He found opportunity staring him in the face. At the end of Alderley Edge High Street there is a shopping parade. Probably built in the 1970s, it is functional but looks a bit tired. He had an instinctive feel that something could be done here. So he took action, in typical Andy White fashion.

'The word was that the owner wouldn't sell it to anybody. I found out who he was and went down to his house unannounced. I knocked on his door. He was a chap in London now in his eighties. I sat down with him and on a piece of A4 paper, I worked out how much I thought I could afford to pay as a development site.'

Andy's magic with people kicked in again and having worked out what the site was worth, they shook hands on the deal. There was just one minor problem which Andy had not considered particularly relevant during his negotiations. He didn't have any money.

He instructed lawyers, knowing that he didn't have the money to pay them either, and treated this lack of funds as if it were just a minor detail. He went and found an investment partner on the basis of a 50:50 split of the profits. In time he got planning consent for a redevelopment which would increase the density on the site fivefold. As a result, the value of the site went up threefold. Bang. He was back in business. It could take up to four years from start to finish before he cashes in on this scheme, and although he says he is spending more time at home, opportunities keep presenting themselves and he is finding it hard to resist.

One Sunday afternoon in the Wacky Warehouse watching his son in the soft play area, a friend got him thinking. He said, 'Andy, you need something to occupy your mind. What would you do if you had the choice and the money?' He remembered a scheme he had been involved in four years earlier in Kings Lynn, where they had bought a property with an income stream to increase the yield, better the planning consent and then sell or redevelop. He thought that he would quite like to do that, but it required a lot of cash.

A few weeks later he was helping out another friend with a business problem, when he was asked a rather vague question. 'Would you fancy doing something with a group of people I know, because I know they will want to work with you?' Andy asked what it was. He was intrigued by the reply: 'You tell us.'

He developed an idea, based on scaling up the Kings Lynn type of scheme that he had been thinking of. He went to meet the people – two members of the House of Lords and a small group of wealthy businessmen. They put a team together to begin to take forward this idea.

One of the group rang Andy from Spain one Friday morning and told him to go and meet the bank; they were interested in the idea. After six weeks of grilling and interrogation, the bank had become convinced that the concept could work, and they asked the question 'How much do you want?' The reply was swift. 'Two hundred and fifty million.' The bank came in as an equity partner; now it was time to go to work.

The idea is simple really. Andy explains it like this:

'You tend to find that the majority of people who own property do not actively manage it. Where we score is that we have a team of people dedicated to actively managing that portfolio to sweat it and make it work. Occupancy, rentals, leases; change the leases, re-jig them, improve the properties, increase the rental values, which in turn increases the value. So that's where you make the money. A small tweak makes a big gain.'

You might think that small tweaks cannot make much money, but you have to understand the scale of the operation. Using the war chest secured from the bank, a team was assembled and in April 2006 the action began.

'We had a chance to buy a portfolio for £120 million. The problem we had was credibility. I knew we had a good team behind us, but no credibility because I'd never done it before, nobody knew who we were. We got the opportunity and between the Friday and the Monday I convinced the bloke that was selling to run with us. On the Friday when I first spoke to him he was an arrogant jock but by Sunday night I had worn him down. He said you get me this letter and you are one of the four bidders. We did, and we exchanged and completed within 27 days – £120 million. From nothing to £120million in a short space of time, that has subsequently increased to £175 million. We are just about to increase it again by another £150million, by

114

adding on portfolios. We now own 21 properties between Sunderland and the City of London.'

***

Working with the bank as a partner, the plan is to take the portfolio to £1 billion within the next three years, which Andy is confident they will do. He loves the style of working; it is totally the opposite of the way the corporate world works. He says:

> 'We've got a good team. We don't employ a single person. Everything is outsourced, and as we sit here today, the portfolio has gone up by £25million in value.'

***

Though he is spending more time at home, he continues to respond to the itch that he can't scratch.

> 'We've got a team of people together with a brief to see where opportunities lie. Underperforming sectors, sectors where there could be consolidation, people whose businesses are suffering for whatever reason, people who require extra management, people who are looking to sell a business. We are just about to put shareholders together to move that forward.'

***

Now he is concentrating on putting controls and procedures in place so he can free up his mind for other things. What kind of other things? He smiles.

> 'I used to do a bit of stand-up comedy when I was potless. I want to do more stand-up comedy, singing, writing, enjoy my family, be happy, make a few quid, make people laugh, that's about it really. You know; life. It's the best thing that ever happened to me.'

***

Those are great goals to have. One has to wonder though, if a man like Andy White can enjoy such an idyllic existence, because tomorrow is another day and he knows how he will feel when he wakes up in the morning.

> 'Every morning when you wake up, you have to think like the gazelle. The gazelle has got to run like fuck to keep out of the way of the lion, so every day when you wake up keep running like that gazelle.'

***

It is a pretty safe bet that come the morning Andy White will be running again whether he needs to or not.

Before he runs, I ask him for a tip for success. He says 'Drink water. It's good enough for lions.'

Perhaps the Maverick was meant to be a comedian after all.

Entrepreneurial insights from the Maverick

- Be a people person – we may not all be stand-up comedians, but we can all take the time and trouble to try to better the lives of the people we are working with. Andy White's genuine love of people shines through. It is not an act; he wants to do whatever he can to make a difference. The commitment and buy-in he gets because of this attitude has enabled him to get things done against all the odds; win business that he has no right to win; and to become a magnet for opportunity.

- Set goals – in Andy's experience few people explicitly set out their goals for their career or their life. Think about them, prioritize them, set times-cales against them and take action.

- Use your intuition – if you have belief in yourself and what you are doing, tune into your intuition. Malcolm Gladwell, in his book *Blink*, suggests that decisions made very quickly can be every bit as good as decisions made cautiously and deliberately, by tuning into our adaptive uncon-sciousness. He calls it the 'power of the glance'. Andy puts such trust in his business intuition that he is willing to set out multi-million pound deals on beer mats and scraps of paper.

- Keep your feet on the ground – when you start to believe your own hype you are in trouble. No matter how big your business gets, stay close to real people. Listen to the cleaner, say thank you to your staff, and know the price of a gallon of petrol.

- Laugh. Whether you are up or you are down, laugh. It's good for you.

10

The Magic Bean

'There is some business we will not do because it makes us sad.'

There was a time when companies would give Luncheon Vouchers as a mark of the value that they placed upon their employees. Many companies have not moved on from this position. Their employees, in truth, are about as valued as a limp sandwich wrapped in cling film.

The Magic Bean sees things differently. Her employees are given group psychotherapy sessions, they have a life coach, and every year they are given their own budget to spend on personal development. They can spend it on anything that they think will help them to grow as people and as ethical professionals. They can meditate in a Himalayan temple, learn to do magic or just go on course. Whatever it is that they want to do.

Elaine James is the Magic Bean. She is an ethical entrepreneur. She has an unusual way of looking at the world of business, which has its roots in her strong moral code and her experience of seeing people treated badly in the name of profit.

She likes to make money and knows how to do it. She demands to be paid handsomely for a job done amazingly. Then she gives a lot of her money away. She earns from the rich to give to the poor, and in the process helps the rich to become more ethical and responsible.

She sees herself as a Magic Bean, just like the makuna bean. It can root itself on barren land. It grows very quickly and produces heavy foliage. When it rots down it leaves a fertile soil so that other things can grow.

Today, this is a rather unusual approach to business. However, with businesses being encouraged to be more ethical, more sustainable, more socially responsible, don't be surprised if in ten years' time every business runs on Magic Bean principles.

It's an approach which owes much to the Koan, which is why Elaine calls her company by that name. So what is the Koan?

It is a paradoxical question; a catalyst for awakening one's true nature; a can-opener for the heart and mind.

Prepare to have your mind opened and your heart warmed. This is a story of the inherent goodness of people.

Take me to the Koan

It is well documented in research that male entrepreneurs are driven by their need to escape from their feelings of separation. Female entrepreneurs generally tend to be better educated and driven by the need for self actualization, to find fulfilment within themselves. Unlike many male entrepreneurs, women can often achieve fulfilment within business and then, if they want to, stop and move on to the next thing in their lives, feeling satisfied they have done a good job.

Elaine James, the Magic Bean, concurs; she says:

'It's not like a chase for me. I could stop. I can totally relate to the idea about women having a passion about something. I'm already planning what I am going to do when I'm old and it's not this. The business was about self actualization. It was about learning about myself and forcing myself to be around others and be part of a team.'

In doing so she has created a business which deals in ethical public relations, organizational development and endows part of its profits to its own Magic Bean Charitable Trust, as well as setting up a fund to help people get new enterprising ideas off the ground. It is a values-driven business which believes in looking after its staff and its clients as well as taking small actions to create a better world and help other people. A lot of people just don't understand this approach. Elaine says:

'Sometimes I've had to be quite tough and stick to my guns when other people were telling me I was a fruit loop. They said, "That's not the way you do it". I said, "Well, actually it's the way that I'm going to do it".'

So she did. She set out her business on the basis that it would be true to its values, and, as such, some things are non-negotiable. Even if it meant that profits would be reduced, she would not compromise her values. Perversely, this value-driven approach is actually helping to increase profits, and after four years of laying the foundations of the company, it now turns over more than £1 million and is perfectly positioned to ride the wave of ethical business. As Marks & Spencer and Tesco have recently taken a strong ethical stance, the rest of the corporate world is ready to follow and Koan is poised to grow like the proverbial Magic Bean.

This open, refreshing, honest, ethical business took root when Elaine reached her lowest ebb. She had burned herself out and been crushed by the corporate world, lost her mother after a five year battle against cancer and got divorced. She was totally drained. Not wanting to end up 'A f***** up thirty something' she started a programme of psychotherapy.

Looking over the Edge

Elaine was an enthusiastic and ambitious girl from a mill town working class family. There was a very strong work ethic in her family, and Elaine worked from the age of thirteen, taking part time shop jobs for a pound an hour.

On her eighteenth birthday, her sister sold her bike so that she could buy Elaine a birthday present. She came home bikeless, carrying a book. She says:

> 'It was Anita Roddick's, *Body and Soul – How to Succeed in Business & Change the World*. I sat on my bed and read it. I thought here's this woman, she's not wearing a power suit, she is doing something really good, and clearly she's making some money in doing it.'

It was to have a lasting effect on Elaine. She felt inspired by this woman, but there was no time to do anything about it then: she had an education to get.

She was the first person in her family to go to university, and though her parents were supportive, she found it quite an isolating experience. She remembers:

> 'I did a degree in the History of Design in the Visual Arts, which sounds a bit bizarre. The core of it was about society and people and how often art imitated life and vice versa. Not only art but looking at design and how it reflected life and what was happening at the time. I loved the society aspect of it. My mum and dad often said to me, "What is it that you are doing again?" They were very supportive but couldn't fully understand it.'

She didn't do very well in the exams, and years later she understood one of the reasons why. Her daughter was diagnosed as slightly dyslexic and Elaine was too. So with not a very good degree in an off-the-wall subject, what do you do?

'I went to work for a control and instrumentation company. It was not very glamorous and it was a bit dull. They made thermostatic controls, gauges and meters. But I sat next to the woman who did PR and began to get interested in it. She left after about six months and I went to the Managing Director and said "Please can I have her job? I'm really ignited by it. It's really interesting".'

The MD had a value system of his own. He considered Elaine's plea for all of a moment and said, 'You are too young and anyway, I want a man for the job.' With selection criteria like this, it was a wonder he kept any staff. He certainly wasn't going to keep Elaine.

'It annoyed me. I was only a whippersnapper of about twenty-three, and I thought, "Well, that's not on". So I looked to the ad agency that worked for them, approached them and said, "I think you need a PR department; that's the way things are going". Looking back I knew nothing, but I was confident, threw myself in and they said "OK". I had to learn very, very quickly.'

So off she went to set up a new PR department for the ad agency her now ex-employers had used. She admits she was making it up as she went along, speaking to people and honing her craft. It wasn't very sexy. In the early days she was writing and talking to the media about construction. She was not the kind of person to get stuck with at parties: she could tell you all about backhoe loaders and fluoroelastemers. She was getting pretty good at this, but felt that the agency were just going through the motions with it, so at twenty-four she walked out and set herself up in business. That wasn't very sexy either.

'My first job was for Wormald Ansell Firespring closures. I remember that very well. I knew a lot about protection and suppression systems.'

You can imagine the party invitations were a bit thin on the ground.

Crushed

Elaine was doing well but she began to reflect on what it was that she really wanted:

'I thought, if I do this for the next ten years, it will only ever be so big in terms of personal fulfilment. I wanted to work with consumer brands, I wanted to travel, I wanted to be at the helm. I'm tentative about saying "in charge"; I wanted to direct things rather than ruling over them.'

Connect Point, a Manchester Advertising Agency, was hungry for growth, both organically and through acquisition. They had noticed Elaine and invited her to set up a PR company in which she would be a shareholder. It offered her everything she had wished for, so off she went.

She grew it very successfully.

'I was the Managing Director at just twenty-seven. I was responsible for employing people, managing, business strategy and client accounts. It was a big responsibility. I thought I was really grown up. Now I know better.'

She was certainly single-minded and driven, and with the success she took some hard knocks. She realizes now that she didn't understand herself very well at the time and as a consequence couldn't understand other people well enough in order to get the best out of them. Her driven nature meant that she didn't always recognize when personal issues had a knock-on effect in business.

Then she had a wake-up call. The team she had created turned on her. There was a kind of *coup d'etat*. She says:

'The business imploded. The team imploded. We were twelve people by now. The team pretty much imploded for lots of reasons. It was a micro of what was going on in the group because people weren't treated well. I felt like I'd been couped. There were two people, who were women actually, who were not supportive of me as a woman in business who had a child as well. I came in early and worked over and above when I got home, but I had to leave at 5pm to collect my child from child care. They used that as a lever.'

She was undermined and stabbed in the back in what was really a mini-revolt against her, but she feels it was a result of the company's absence of a people-centred value system.

Elaine told the two women that they were welcome to run the business and moved to become New Business Development Director for the group. Being stabbed in the back was one of the reasons she made the move, but there were other things going on as well. She says:

> 'One, I was incredibly tired. I'd nursed Mum for five years, got divorced, weathered the ups and downs of business issues. I needed some space to reassess things. If I wasn't careful I was going to end up a fucked-up thirty something, so I embarked on psychotherapy with a brilliant therapist. I still go for personal development as much as anything else, it is never ending. Life's biggest challenge is to know oneself. That began to help, and it began to shine some light on why I had worked so hard and so blindly.'

Elaine discovered the hard, focused drive she had always felt was partly a result of not receiving male acknowledgement from her father. She was driving herself and everybody around her in a vain attempt to get a man to say, 'Well done'. She reflects on this.

> 'I'd been socialized to believe that women are dutiful, responsible, put themselves down the queue, and all of those things had led me to behave in a certain way in business. To succeed in business, I've done some really hard work on myself.'

As the psychotherapy progressed she began to get to know herself a lot better. She remembered how inspired she had been when she read the book by Anita Roddick, and she began to play about with some thoughts. These thoughts eventually ended up on a scrap of paper, and they pointed to a new path. She says:

> 'I still have the original scribble pad where I had written down what the business would look like. I got to the point where I knew myself a bit better and I couldn't carry on doing my job because I wasn't being true to myself.
>
> 'So I went in and said, "I can't stay anymore, these are the reasons. I'm happy to sell back the shares. I don't want to fall out with you. There is stuff that I have to go and figure out".'

So with a six-month restrictive covenant in her employment contract, she had some time to sit and figure things out.

'I did some planning, and being a person who is essentially moral and ethical, there is no way I would think about taking clients from the business, which is what most breakaways do; they break off pieces of the business.'

She took out a clean sheet of paper and began to imagine how an ethical, values-driven PR agency would work. In the meantime she sold her house and downsized to a flat, paid off her credit card bills, and when all that was done she had just £6000 left. Then she set to work evolving this new way of thinking, this new way of doing business. She had a lot at stake.

'My daughter was eight. That's a big responsibility. It's not as if I had a partner there, I couldn't think, "Well, if it all goes tits up I'll be fine". But it was a good motivation.
'So I did all of that and thought there's no point going to the bank; they will just say I'm mad. So I got a couple of clients bringing in about £2000 a month selling ethical PR.'

That was in 2002, and she still hasn't been to the bank. The business has always generated positive cash flow and has never borrowed. Never gone a penny overdrawn.

A Koan is born

So. Back to this thing; the Koan. Elaine chose this as the name for her new business. She says:

'Koan is a Zen Buddhist word. My therapist is a Buddhist. It is a word he mentioned one day. I looked it up. It's a paradigm that you meditate upon, so it's a thinking thing. I just like the idea of it. You can enquire of Koan, you can think about it. It tells you something. I also thought it doesn't stand for anything in particular.'

A Koan is really a question that forces you to think in a completely different way, which is what Elaine's business does for its clients. Here's a Koan for you to contemplate: 'If you hear a sound when you clap your hands, what is the sound of one hand clapping?' This kind of paradoxical question forces you to question your assumptions, which is where Elaine thought real opportunity lay, getting organizations to take a radical look at how they do things.

She looked at the emerging market landscape and concluded that Koan could carve out a niche selling ethical PR and communications. Companies were beginning to become more conscious of the importance of behaving ethically; they were thinking about their role in achieving sustainability; and corporate social responsibility was well and truly on their agendas.

Elaine also wanted to instil ethical values within her own company. She had seen people treated very badly in the name of profit. She wanted to make profit, but she wanted people to be treated well. She won't insist that her employees work with people that don't share their values just because they are paying. She has even turned business away if it didn't feel right.

> 'Our values are still grounded as a business. There is some business that we just will not do because it makes us sad. If clients treat us really badly, yes it has a cost implication, but I throw it open to the team and they agree that's not the way we want to make money.'

She says that the Co-operative Bank have been doing this for years, turning away from people who don't share their ethical values. In a traditional PR agency, if you had a dysfunctional relationship with a client you would be asked just to stick with it and keep them paying the bills. She feels you have to value yourself and your team more than that. She has had to ring up a client to explain this and he said, 'I cannot argue with anything you said. Hat's off to you.'

Lord Thomas of Macclesfield pioneered the Co-operative Bank's ethical position, and he has become a great ally for Koan and its approach. Elaine's meeting with him happened just by chance, she remembers.

> 'I bumped into him at a function. We were working for Help the Aged and it was quite funny. He was trying to get in through the barrier and he couldn't. He was struggling with his leg so I went over and teased him. I said, "They are very fussy about who they let in here". I told him about what we were doing and he was the man who introduced ethics into the co-op bank 30 years ago, so I kept him informed.'

Lord Thomas is so impressed by Koan he has volunteered himself as a Non-executive Director. He came into the Koan offices and did 'An audience with' type of event. He wowed everybody with his tales of the Victorian philanthropists who were engaged in models of sustainability one hundred years ago. Somewhere along the line, the principles got lost. Now they are coming back again, which is good news for society and great news for Koan.

The notes that Elaine made on a scratch pad have actually been put into practice. She loves what she does, she is making profits, preparing for growth, and doing things that are making her feel proud. She says:

> 'We are working on a particular project that I am so proud of. It is with Marshalls plc, a UK based company manufacturing and supplying a range of landscape products, including paving. We are helping them to develop their sustainability strategy, and how they communicate that externally. We are working with them at the moment on issues around imported sandstone – imports into the UK are on the up but Marshalls work only from audited quarries that don't use child labour, whilst lots of others won't. It's about actually making the consumer aware of this.'

Other projects include Momentum, something that Koan has developed for Midland Mainline, the train operators. It works with secondary school children along the Mainline routes. The young people look at the sustainability issues that they consider important and bring them into the business via company 'champions'. As well as creating an educational experience for the young people, the issues then begin to impact upon the business procedures and behaviours. Another project is with the Children's Safety Education Foundation, developing the organization structures, procedures and behaviours to deliver effective safety messages to parents and children.

Elaine laughs at the thought that some people may perceive them to be 'tree huggers', because of their unusual approach, but she is comfortable in the knowledge that Koan is measured on results and it is delivering the goods. She says:

> 'Everything that we do is measured and analysed. There are standard measures relating to coverage: brand mentions, sectors, target publications and so on. We aim to get, say, five, pieces of national coverage in broadsheets. Then there are other key performance indicators which can be related to a specific project, for instance, if we want to develop partnerships with a prolific NGO, how do we go about achieving that? If we want to make sure that we are delivering back to children and families how are we going to monitor that? If we want to make an impact in personal development how do we measure that?'

Take note Middle England

This, it seems, is the way businesses are going. Elaine sensed this when she set up Koan, and is now totally convinced that it is not just a gentle movement towards ethical business: it is becoming a tidal wave.

> 'At the beginning of this year there was a sea change which I had been expecting because of my research. But when it came I wasn't expecting the scale of it. The retailer Marks & Spencer declared their sustainability policy.'

They were quite certain about it too. Their adverts outlined their ethical values referring to them as 'Plan A', adding, 'There is no Plan B'. In other words: this is it and we are 100% committed to it.

Elaine says:

> 'Hot on the heels of Marks & Spencer's was Tesco. These are mainstream organizations. You know when you go to Marks & Spencer that the sandwich wrapping is made from biodegradable maize. When the buying public is demanding those things you know there is no going back. All the indications are that fair trade and organic sales are going up.'

There is a further challenge which is driving companies towards more ethical ways of doing business. Middle England is waking up. Consumers are more independent and free thinking than ever before; they don't conform to the stereotype that was Middle England. Now there are consumers with conscience who are making lifestyle choices, irrespective of their socio-economic grouping. Add to that the fragmentation of the media, and it represents a real challenge for brands and for organizations. According to Elaine:

> 'Some are going to be left with their heads spinning, thinking "Well, what happened there?" They can't engage with the fact that some fundamental things have changed.'

The Stern Report on the economics of climate change and the associated environmental issues, published in October 2006, is also having an effect on consumer behaviour. But, according to Lord Thomas, 'Business leads': more and more businesses are driving the ethical agenda and consumers are latching on to it.

This is great news if you are, like Koan, in the business of ethical PR, but for Elaine this is a really crucial time in the development of her business.

'At this moment in time it's a modest business. Growth is an aspiration. It's interesting; if we are not careful and don't move quite quickly this year, we will end up having been the market educators on ethics in communication and PR. A lot of people are waking up. We could end up being the ant that gets squashed by the elephant so we are working hard to avoid that.'

Giant strides have been made in the way that companies are latching on to ethical issues. Other traditional companies are beginning to tread into Elaine's niche, and although this is a concern, she counters it with more comforting thoughts. She says:

'It's thinking stuff really. It's not, "Oh you want to sell phones? I'll bang out a few press releases". It's not an easy PR sell, it's not like handbags or hair products, you have to know your stuff, engage with it, have compassion and intelligence. Which is very challenging for the PR industry, I can't find people to employ in the PR industry.'

The chances are if she can't find the right people, neither can the more traditional PR agencies, and their foray into ethical communication may well be short-lived. The other strength Koan has is in the foundations she has laid. She has resisted an all-out dash for growth and turnover in favour of setting things up the way she wants them. She was clear from the outset that she wanted to give something back to society, so she has set up the Magic Beans Charitable Foundation. Then there is Be Magic Ltd, which is an inspirational organizational development arm alongside Koan.

The Magic Beans Charitable Foundation will receive an endowment of between 5% and 10% of company profits each year, which will be spent on good causes. She says:

'We have agreed our first project through a partner organization called the David Sheldrick Wildlife Trust in Northern Tsavo in Africa, which is a sustainable futures project out there. We've made a commitment to fund that.'

Now that the various parts of the business are well established, Elaine reflects on how she did it.

'Creating this business the way I have has been like being a builder or an architect. I feel that I have been building a bigger house than other people might have set out to build. So if you look on the skyline it's not a very high building. But now we've got really strong foundations in place. As the building starts to go up it could be a beautiful mansion, a beautiful place to live. That's how I want my business to be. I think I've seen some people do it in reverse. They grow a business and then want to branch out. I've mapped it out so that it can grow.'

So as she gets ready to move into a higher gear, she still remembers that she has to be up front with everyone. She has never borrowed and so there is still no real relationship with the bank. Growth implies risk and she refers to her employees as risk takers.

'Some of the risk takers that have come into the business, I've always been up front and told them that we were a high risk business. I had to make that clear. So you get brave souls joining me. They don't own a part of the business, but there are two individuals who will eventually have equity. That's being drawn up. Others will benefit from the profitability as well.'

As she prepares to leave, Elaine presents me with her business card. As you might expect, it is an embodiment of the ethical principles of Koan in every way. It is different from any other business card you have seen. It is one quarter of an inch thick for one thing. When you look closely at it you will see that it is a composite of four recycled materials. On the top, there is a coating of pulped cardboard, underneath that there are three layers of recycled rubber, one pink, one amber and one blue. On the pulped cardboard side is the company logo, Koan, but because everybody in Koan is seen as an individual, everyone is free to add a personal touch to the logo on their own business card. Elaine's features a string of magic beans weaving themselves in and out of the letters. On the reverse side, there are some words embossed deep into the blue recycled rubber. The words read:

Elaine James
Change agent, Lover of life
Impish believer in our inherent good &
Ability to make a positive impact.

She is an ambassador for a new breed of ethical entrepreneurs. She is a walking, talking Magic Bean who can open your mind and warm your heart.

Entrepreneurial insights from the Magic Bean

- Having a clear set of values helps you to stay on course. Many businesses don't clarify their values. As a result they often send out confusing messages to both their staff and their clients. When the going gets tough, businesses without clear values, backed up by consistent behaviours, can become volatile, unpredictable and at risk. When you have a well-defined track, even if you come off, you have one to get back on. Clear, unequivocal, shared values are the best track a business can have.

- Put something back. The great entrepreneurs of the Victorian era were often great philanthropists and social reformers too. They balanced their financial success by commitment to fantastic social innovations. Somewhere along the line, this got forgotten. Elaine has created a model that allows her to earn from the rich and give to the poor.

- Look after your people physically, psychologically and economically. Elaine believes that her success is down to her people. She wants to share it by rewarding people and looking after their wider needs. Psychotherapy helps her employees to avoid suppressing issues from work or home which may affect the business; they are encouraged to establish goals both personally and professionally; and they get to decide for themselves what will make them a better person. Well-rounded staff will create a well-rounded business.

11

The Carer

'When I got my first Mercedes I used to hide it. I just felt guilty.'

Karen Coleman felt the tears slowly sliding down her cheeks. Clustering around her chin, a single teardrop fell. She watched as it hit the floor. Next to it another droplet landed. Then another, and another. These droplets were red – blood.

She cried out as she looked at the reddened mess where she had sliced the razor across her wrists.

Luckily for Karen, this was not to be the end. Neither was it to be her beginning. Her turning point in life came much later, but only after she had endured physical abuse; become a teenage mum twice; tried to take her own life; had a tempestuous relationship with her stepfather; financial fallouts with both her mother and her husband; and lost the love of her life in a tragic accident.

Remarkably, unbelievably, not only has she survived, she is the charismatic owner of a business which is attracting the attention of serious buyers and as of today is valued for sale at £8 million.

She is a bundle of energy and optimism – her conversation is frequently punctuated by infectious jovial laughter. After all that has happened to her, she beams as she says, 'It really is time for me to pack a lot into my life now'.

If ever there was a role model for women entrepreneurs, this is it. Her story will inspire and encourage you, whatever odds are stacked against you. It is possible to do more than just survive; it is possible to find yourself and to succeed.

Dockers, Diggle and disruption

Today, the docks in Salford have been regenerated. Where the sugar boats once docked, there are houses for professional types, offices, retail outlets and the iconic home of matchstalk men and matchstalk cats and dogs, The Lowry Centre.

When Karen was born, the docks were booming and employed thousands of men doing hard manual work. Dockers were hard men, and Karen's paternal grandfather Borland was one of them.

Hard on the outside at least. Yet he was also solid, compassionate, loving and tender. In her early years it was grandma and granddad Borland who acted as surrogate parents. She says that this was because her mother was not 'very well balanced', and it was decided that it would be best for everyone.

The terraced house in a cobbled street close to the docks could easily have been a scene from one of Selwyn Demmy's collection of Lowrys. It was the place where Karen felt most at home.

'The most love I have ever received in my entire life was from my grand-ma who died when I was four and my granddad.

'He was a tough nut. A hard Salford docker. He used to let me curl his hair with rollers. I was brought up with love. No money just love.'

When Karen was nine, her loving environment was shattered. Her mother had remarried and took Karen to live with her and the new stepfather. Saddleworth near Oldham was to be her new home and she was sent to school in nearby Diggle.

Her troubles were about to begin. From that moment, her stepfather began a pattern of physical and mental abuse which was to haunt Karen for much of her life. In addition to the abuse she was made to work from an early age.

'My mum always made me do jobs when I came home from school so I was always aware of work to a degree which is ridiculous. Since I had therapy I can give myself a break now. Even on holiday.'

Karen's mother was an enigma. She was incapable of showing any feelings towards her daughter, yet she was a charismatic whirlwind who became a face on the Manchester social scene.

Karen recalls:

'She was stunning, a beauty queen and a model. She was outrageous. She was notorious and had affairs with quite powerful men. She was an awful mother but charismatic and a grafter. A worker. I've never seen anyone work so hard and look so good. I haven't got her energy.'

In her own enigmatic style, she would be letting a house to eight students one moment, be renovating and decorating another house, have a full-time job and always have an affair on the go. She never went anywhere before she had smoked a cigarette and put her full make-up on. She always dressed the part, whether she was doing crazy paving or modelling, and men just loved her. In Karen's eyes she was both devious and materialistic.

Karen was hardly even on her mother's radar screen, and it is hard to believe that an amazing character like Karen Coleman describes herself as shy, but she does.

'At secondary school I was quite a shy person. Alcohol loosens my tongue and makes me feel confident. I'm confident in business, yet in my personal life I'm still awful.' She guffaws with laughter as she describes her coping strategy. 'I just turn into a fruit bat!'

By the time she was fifteen, the systematic abuse and the absence of any love was breaking her apart and her behaviour became more and more disruptive.

'I turned into a rebel without a cause. I was awful. I was drinking, smoking, having underage sex, being disruptive, an absolute nightmare.'

Then she made a decision. She was going to get pregnant at just fifteen. So she did. At the time she had thought this through as best she could.

'I was so unhappy and all I wanted in my little pea brain, then, was to have a happy family, the way it should be.'

She thought that a baby would bring her the happiness she so longed for. However, she suffered severe post natal depression, which at the time went undiagnosed and untreated. It was then that she hit rock bottom and made her attempt to end her life.

Yet, through it all, the only consistent thing was her work ethic. When she married, her husband was unemployed and, in Karen's words, a 'bit wet'. She had a job at the plastics factory and cooked, washed and cleaned. She did whatever she had to do to bring in some money.

Soon afterwards she gave up the baby, a girl, to the father who, along with his parents, raised her. Karen was barely in a fit state to look after herself, let alone a baby.

When eventually Karen was given medication, she spoke to a solicitor to try to get the child back, but she was told that it was pointless as she did not have a stable home. She finds it ironic that this was the case. She was renting one of her mother's cottages. Her mother was good at collecting the rent money but offered Karen no support whatsoever.

'My mother was living in a sixteen bedroom house and driving a Jag but she was too busy having affairs.'

Out of the frying pan into the fire

Desperate for love and affection, Karen began a phase in her life which she describes as 'Promiscuous, promiscuous, promiscuous'. She imagined that if she looked as good as she could and gave as good as she could then she would end up being secure and happy. She says:

'That's all I wanted, it's what I still want.'

Still, by this time she had learned that contraception would be a good idea, and she began taking a contraceptive pill. But she was sick a lot, and for a second time, aged just eighteen, she fell pregnant. She recalls it with incredulity.

'I'm on the pill and I get pregnant, that's the truth. The doctor says, "You're pregnant." I said, "Jesus!"'

It wasn't as though this was her only problem. Her mother had begun a new relationship with a police officer. According to Karen he was a 'maniac character'. She says:

'I was going through a bad time and just didn't get enough support, but I thought, "Well, Mother's happy". I was more supportive to her than she was to me.'

Karen's mum bought her partner a business, a café in Ashton-under-Lyne. He was unsuited to this new role; the café soon floundered and Karen's mum quickly showed her ruthless streak. She took Karen to the bank and helped her secure a loan so that she could buy the café from her mother. It was losing money, Karen was saddled with an ailing business, a bank loan and on top of this she found herself pregnant by a man that she describes as an 'obnoxious criminal gangster'.

You might think that this would be the cue for a mother and daughter reconciliation. A turning point in their relationship. No such luck. Karen's mum had bought a busy pub. Who better to keep it going than a penniless, homeless, single mother with a work ethic bordering on psychosis?

To cope, she did what her mother had hoped she would do. She threw herself headlong into a working frenzy. The pub was next to Culdrose airbase and had three types of clientele. There were the locals, genuine ordinary people. People who Karen found a natural affinity with. Secondly, there were the holidaymakers who brought variety and interest to the village. And then there were the airmen.

In Karen, the airmen found someone who they could banter with, and she began a new round of liaisons. Perhaps sensing her growing confidence and power, she only dated officers.

One evening, a strikingly handsome officer walked into the pub. He was a young Irishman called Mark, who seemed somewhat different from the crowd. He was slightly aloof and on the periphery, often making him the butt of the jokes from his fellow officers.

She still struggles as she thinks of him.

'I say to this day Mark was the love of my life. I would have died for him. A lovely man and I'm still in touch with his mother. I met Mark and fell absolutely, madly, besottedly, blindly in love. He was extremely good looking. Drop dead gorgeous, but aloof as well.'

Mark had served in the Falklands on HMS Invincible and came home unscathed. On his return, he bought himself a motorbike. In Ireland, he'd been a keen and fairly successful racer. Speed was his thing. It was his real excitement. His drug.

All of his friends worried about him and warned him about the way he rode that bike. Yet it was his release. His reason for being. Then one day on a country lane he just pushed it too hard. It was a tragic accident and a great loss. Mark was no more.

For a single mother who had found the love she craved, it was yet another battle she had to overcome. There was no bereavement counselling. Her mother didn't even allow her any time off work.

Once again, Karen threw herself headlong into working.

'I used to work six days and six nights a week, cleaning, cooking, bar work, everything. Hard graft, and I had my son as well.'

It took its toll.

'I drank far too much. Even though I hadn't had any education and always felt inferior to people, I suddenly realized that actually I was far brighter than all of these people put together.'

Nine months after Mark's tragic accident, she finally began to grieve and really feel the pain. She decided it would be better to return to the North West, renting a flat above a greengrocery. She had no fears about providing for her son because if there was one thing she knew how to do, it was work. She worked in a plastics factory; a hotel; a pub; and did cleaning jobs.

Then she fell into something which in time would give meaning to her life and launch her.

That something was caring. She took a low-paid job in a care home. Her experience in the pub in Cornwall had developed her natural ability to deal with all kinds of people and her confidence and belief in herself was growing.

What's more, all she wanted in life was to give love and get some back. Here she was able to do it and get paid for it. Unexpectedly, she had stumbled upon something that she loved.

Love saves the day

Yet things couldn't go smoothly for Karen. Enter Razi, an Iranian dentist. They married. She for love, he, she says, for a UK residential visa. Yet they stayed together for fourteen years.

Meanwhile Karen had got wind that the agency she worked for was for sale and approached her mother who raised the finance. In a single day, Karen went from working in a care home to owning the business. She knew nothing whatsoever about business, but her passion for caring meant that she was growing it rapidly. Her mother, meanwhile, was milking the business of its profits. Karen, in her naivety, had concentrated on care; she hadn't given a second thought to looking after the profits she was generating.

On top of this, her mother and Razi hated each other and inevitably there was a massive fallout. The agency was sold, and Karen emerged with just £22,000. It seemed Razi had big plans for the cash.

He suggested that they buy a takeaway business. Karen got it going and worked fourteen hours a day, seven days a week. Meanwhile, Razi liked his Armani suits and fast cars. She was working every hour God sent and yet she was still losing money.

Finally, Karen decided it was time she did something for herself. She went upstairs to the flat above the takeaway, ordered two phone lines and £200 worth of old second-hand furniture. She still keeps, as a memento, one of the old brown chairs that she bought.

She realized that she had the ingredients to create a business. She knew how care homes worked; she had experience; and she had a few connections. What's more, she cared about caring.

Everything was done on a shoestring. Then, one day, the phone rang. It was to be a phone call which would be the start of a business which today has a turnover of £15 million a year. She remembers it well.

'It was weird because I got a call from a nursing home in Ashton-under-Lyne via Yellow Pages. It was this "fuddy duddy" old people's home. They gave us a five-day nine-'til-five Registered General Nurse contract.

'There was a lovely-looking Australian nurse who had just come over and she was looking for a job. We paid six weeks in arrears at the time. She didn't want to go, but I implored her and eventually she went. She hated it but stayed nine weeks.'

And so it began. Typically she didn't rest on her laurels; she worked harder and harder.

'The first seven years I sat my arse down on the chair virtually 24/7. I hardly took any holidays. The first couple of years I had to do the on-call throughout the night.

'We didn't have fancy brochures. Some of my early stuff, letters, marketing material – I can laugh now – but – because of my slight dyslexia – was full of spelling mistakes and some was even handwritten.'

This didn't seem to matter, because she was realizing that she had a remarkable ability to communicate with all kinds of people. She never forgot her years of working as a carer, which meant her philosophy was one of care and attention in all matters, particularly relating to staff, something quite unusual for a care agency in those days.

What really drove her business was what still drives it today: she didn't really think too much about the money. She really, genuinely, deeply cares about the end product – caring for people. Service users, customers and staff all have their own needs. Because she focused on this she was able to match supply and demand more consistently and to a level of quality which began to give the established players in the industry the jitters.

They were right to feel threatened. They were going through the motions, whilst Karen began to think more and more about what the business was about and how she could improve it. Because she cared so passionately about her staff, hers was the first agency in the country to set up its own three-stage training programme, making her staff more confident, more competent, more able to progress professionally and achieve higher earnings, as well as giving them a sense of being valued.

This was an extra cost, which came out of her bottom line, which was why her competitors were not too keen to follow suit. They should have taken more notice, because she was able to attract the best staff and keep them longer. In doing so, she slowly but surely began to brush the competition aside. Today, her company, APEX, is the largest independent care agency in the UK, and soon will begin its expansion from its North West base into Yorkshire and the Midlands.

Today, all agencies are required through legislation to have a programme like the one Karen set up long ago on her own initiative. Even though she now has a management team running a £15 million business, she continues to stress to all her staff what the business is about:

> 'We are an agency but APEX cares. I try to get this across to everybody: we are not a conveyor belt turning out beans, we are a nursing and care agency that is professional. The care element of our business is essential to keep at the forefront.'

She feels that one of the secrets of her success in growing the business has been her commitment to choosing hands-on, practical people to join her management team. All of them, with the exception of the finance director, started on the front line, either working as a carer or in one of her call centre operations. She's really proud when she says:

'My managing director could go out and deliver care on Christmas day if he had to. I've had loads of tossers; the sort of people that go to our competitors; theory people. Our business has maintained its consistency by being practical, not theoretical. Most people who grow anything forget very quickly where they came from.'

In the early days, margins were high, but the care industry has become highly regulated. On the plus side, it means that the barriers to entry now are very high, and the industry is beginning to consolidate into fewer and larger providers. The downside is that profit margins are being eroded by the increased costs involved in achieving highly regulated quality standards, the costs of vetting staff, and slow payment from customers. In addition, an intensely competitive arena is being generated by the public sector: e-auctions mean firms are made to bid against each other for work online; the NHS's new right to cancel a contract with just four hours notice; and the creation of a new, not-for-profit agency, 'NHS Professionals', all mean the landscape has changed dramatically.

These are tough times for the industry, yet Karen is buoyant. Though she says she knows very little about business and nearly collapsed the first time she saw a tender document, she is again showing the optimism and foresight that is the mark of the entrepreneur.

She has set up a new company which will do two things. APEX currently has seven offices and is expanding into new areas. Only one of the offices is owned by APEX; the rest are leased. Karen's new firm will firstly buy the offices and rent them to APEX, so that instead of paying someone else rent, she will be paying herself. Secondly, it makes it possible to enter the market for providing supported living. This is specialist accommodation for people with learning disabilities and people with mental health problems which has with it a package of care. The new company will provide the accommodation and maintain it, whilst APEX will provide the care staff, getting it into more long-term contracts. It also gives her more control over the quality of the whole operation, something, she says, 'That makes me happy and satisfied'.

Karen will sell the APEX business sometime soon for something in the region of £8 million, and the new company will provide a revenue stream for her in future years.

Dare to stop

According to research, for the out-and-out male entrepreneur, stopping is impossible. They have an itch that they will never be able to scratch.

Women sometimes become entrepreneurs for different reasons. It can be more about self actualization, achieving something that they care about. When they feel they have done it, they are able to quite happily stop, congratulate themselves and move on to some other interest.

That's good news for Karen, because she was almost stopped before she got to this stage. She recalls what happened when the business really started to take off:

'I went through a lot of stress because I'm not a business person. Even though the business was very, very successful, I went through years of feeling fearful and out of control. I've been gullible and naïve and had loads of people rip me off. One of the reasons is that I was so desperate to get some support.

'As it grew, it was getting harder. I became control freakish. I had a complete nervous breakdown and ended up in the Priory Clinic. I was driving home one night, I'd been working round the clock and I was on a weird diet too. I know now that I was having a panic attack. I got all these weird feelings in my arms I felt spaced out and I thought, "I'm going". It was as simple as that. "I'm going". I still get them but I can control them.

'I was driving myself mad. I was a perfectionist. What I've learned is that perfectionist behaviour is impossible because there is no such thing as perfection.

'I just became sick. Agoraphobic, claustrophobic, hypochondriac. I was house bound. I was in coronary care. I do not underestimate stress or the brain anymore. It took 18 months to get to some normal lifestyle and then five years to feel normal again.'

Success has not come easy for Karen, and it is hard to think of someone that deserves it more.

As she begins to think about what she might do in the future, she contemplates Voluntary Service Overseas, but then reconsiders. One reason is that she doesn't think she would like to go for a year, and secondly she wonders if her talents are needed closer to home.

'The other side of me says that you don't have to go to Africa. There are loads of bloody things that need fixing in this country. I want to do things and pursue them. I don't give a shit about money. I spend most of it on other people anyway.

'Money is not my driver. Yes, I do buy weird handbags and things and have a nice car, but it's not my driver. Not now, not ever.'

As Karen prepares for the next phase of her quite remarkable life, she is beginning to think about the social issues that she might turn her attention to. Issues where politicians, with their theoretical view of the world, have failed.

Few people have experienced as much in life as Karen Coleman. She has a lot to give, and she will give it in her own inimitable style.

Watch out, world.

Entrepreneurial insights from the Carer

- Not having an education is no barrier to success. Remember that Karen left school at fifteen and with no qualifications.

- Entrepreneurs succeed regardless of the resources available to them. A flat above a takeaway, two phone lines and some beat up old furniture enabled Karen to apply her natural resources – communication, insight and an insatiable work ethic.

- Focus on something that you really care about. If all you care about is money, chances are that people will see through you and avoid you. Even today, Karen cares more about caring than the money. The essence of it seems to be 'concentrate on what's important and the rest will look after itself'.

- Set high standards in everything you do, but take note of Karen's experience. Perfectionism should carry a government health warning. It can kill you. She should know – it almost did.

12

The Bubbleboy

'You can get the bog standard Cristal for £190 a bottle. We don't want to rip people off.'

Cheshire's Mottram Hall Hotel is the venue for the Boodle & Dunthorne Tennis Legends Event. It's a kind of Wimbledon of the North, yet it is more of a party than a competition. Nobody really cares who wins.

Usually it is played out in brilliant sunshine. The ladies are dressed to kill, strawberries and cream and, of course, champagne are the order of the day. Even with global warming though, sunshine cannot be guaranteed, and the Tennis Legends event of 2002 was a wash out.

In the Garden Room at Mottram Hall, the legends of 2002 are growing restless. Temperamental Romanian, Ile Nastase, sits brooding in the corner; Henri Leconte and Mats Wilander stand together, staring forlornly into the rain; whilst Ross Case and Peter MacNamara share yet another pot of tea. Somebody is going to blow a fuse soon. The depressing rain and the constant sitting around, waiting for a break in the weather, are taking their toll. A tension is beginning to prevail.

A seventeen-year-old trainee events manager by the name of Lee Mason has been asked to look after the players' lounge that is the Garden Room. He stands attentively in the corner, surveys the sorry scene and senses the tension in the air. For a moment his boss thinks that the kid has bottled it. He watches as the lad trudges out into the rain. Where the hell is he going? What on earth is the kid doing?

The kid flies up the hotel drive in a golf buggy. It looks like he has lost his marbles and the kid's career is going to be short-lived. The boss stares out into the rain, fuming.

Fifteen minutes later, the boss looks down from an upstairs window. The golf buggy comes to an abrupt halt below. A soaking wet and bedraggled Lee Mason is pulling something off the back of the buggy.

When the boss arrives back in the Garden Room, two former Wimbledon champions are on their feet, flying this way and that, chasing a ping pong ball with tiny bats. The other players gather around a beat up old table tennis table which sags in the middle. They are laughing and shouting and cheering. The table belongs to Lee Mason, The Bubbleboy. He had taken the golf buggy home to get it.

This inspired stroke of initiative transformed the atmosphere in the room. Lee once again stands attentively and quietly in the corner, happy that he has been able to help. Meanwhile the Tennis Legends are like kids at Christmas.

The boss approves. The kid has been noticed.

The apprentice

Lee Mason, the Bubbleboy, is perhaps the youngest and newest recruit to the enterprising world that is the Golden Triangle. In business terms, he is barely out of nappies, yet he has established a thriving business right in the heart of Alderley Edge. It is called The Bubble Room, a restaurant and bar which he set up at the tender age of twenty. It has exceeded everybody's expectations, including his own, and now, having launched himself and begun to flex his enterprising muscles, he is beginning to think big.

For somebody who is learning about enterprise as he goes along, the Bubbleboy could not be in a better place. His bar is like a social club for entrepreneurs. Glance around and you will see the Hustler in the corner nursing his camomile tea; laughter cascades across the room as the Prince tunes into a small group of women; the Maverick sinks his pint of Guinness before flying off to yet another deal; whilst the Thinker sits in his customary seat by the window. He is staring vacantly into space. Something is about to click.

Quite by accident, Lee Mason has created for himself the perfect learning environment. **It's a bit like having the best brains from Harvard Business School sitting in your living room. Except these are not professors with interesting theories of how the world ought to work. These are practical entrepreneurs who bend the world and make it work for them.**

For an apprentice entrepreneur, surely there is no better place to be. The Bubbleboy couldn't agree more.

'I'm working ninety hours a week. I don't have to. I just love it. I love being here.'

He is unusual in that his enterprising nature doesn't seem to be driven by disadvantage. He comes from a comfortable family background and his father has a successful architectural practice, though Lee never really took to school. He says:

'I think my school life was average, more than anything. I've always enjoyed the hands-on approach. At school, I did art and technology and those types of things, rather than computer or writing work.'

As soon as he was old enough, he took a part-time job at Mottram Hall Hotel; and when he went to college he realized that he much preferred working and dropped out after just six months. Academia just wasn't for him. He was well liked at Mottram Hall and they made his part-time position into a full-time one, making him an events assistant.

He was pleased. He says:

'It was local for me, and I've always been interested in the service industry, catering and bars. Mottram Hall, when I was 15–16, was really quite glamorous, all the footballers were going, so I said to myself, "Let's see what can happen here".'

Lee's father had spent thirty years as an architect designing bars and restaurants, so Lee had grown up surrounded by ideas and concepts related to the hospitality industry. This really caught his imagination.

'I thought, this is something I could see myself doing. I love customer service, interaction, meeting different people.'

So he applied himself diligently to his duties at Mottram Hall. By the time he reached the grand age of eighteen he was Team Leader running all the events and weddings, including the Tennis Legends events where he had first got himself noticed as a kid who liked to please. Still at just eighteen years of age, he became the Duty Manager. He remembers:

'I was the Duty Manager at the hotel at eighteen, with a £20 million hotel under my control at certain times. From that, I thought this must be something which I'm good at.'

A year later, he was put in charge of all the other team leaders, managing people who were in their late twenties, many with university degrees in business studies and hospitality management. That didn't seem to bother Lee. His concern was just about getting things right for the customer – oh, and dreaming dreams that one day he would have a place of his own to run.

He didn't have to wait long.

Think Bubbles

The offices of the Mason Architectural Practice looked out onto an Italian restaurant called Si. It was quite a small place, the kind of place that ought to be able to sustain a marginal business. But over the years, various marginal businesses had come and gone as sooner or later the margins tipped the wrong way. Si had closed; before that, another restaurant, Siro's, called time; and before Siro's, October's had put up the shutters.

Surely, anyone taking on these premises should call it 'the Lemon', because in business terms it was just that.

As an architect, though, Lee's father, Mark Mason, saw something else and suggested to Lee that he go and have a look at it. The place had nothing going for it. It was small, narrow, was divided into a front and a back, and had been the home to one unsuccessful business after another. Surely this was not the place for a kid with no qualifications to start his first enterprise.

Yet Lee was excited. He could see beyond the grease and the tacky furniture that Si had left behind. He could see his future beginning to unfold. He remembers:

> 'We came and viewed the place and thought it could work for what we wanted. We didn't want anything too big too soon; we wanted to see how it could go. I had all my ideas for service and the background of training from Mottram Hall.'

Lee's father's background was to complement this operational know-how. He had re-designed the Yates Wine Lodge chain and worked on cool bars like Revolution and Dogma, which are located throughout the UK.

Around the kitchen table at home, a 'think bubbles' concept began to emerge, with mum chipping in with thoughts about the interior look and design.

It is quite a quirky concept, which may be one of the reasons why it works. By day it has a cosy feel, almost like a casual gentleman's club. Large leather armchairs of various shapes and sizes are assembled around a room, which in truth is not much bigger than a living room. Log ends give a rustic feel to some of the walls, whilst others have open brick facings. Italianate tables and lamps sit next to iron girders. It is the opposite of anything that a corporate chain would create. It is eccentric, eclectic and atmospheric.

By night you would be hard pushed to see any of this. The Bubble Room, for all its cramped quirkiness, is packed wall-to-wall with people. Elbow upon elbow of jostling, jovial people, enjoying a night out in Alderley Edge.

In the back room, a thirty-seat restaurant was to be the main thrust of the Bubble Room concept. The bar area was intended as a place where diners could go after their meal and have a quiet drink, whilst the odd local could pop in for a relaxing drink or two. That was the original business model, anyway.

Almost immediately, the business plans and projections had to be torn up. Despite being based upon benchmarks taken from other similar-sized establishments, the projections proved to be hopelessly out of line. They grossly underestimated what was about to happen. They didn't take account of something that you won't learn at any business school. They didn't consider the elbow test.

You've got to pass the elbow test

For years, I have been telling bar owners about the elbow test. Usually they look at me as if I have had too much to drink. One manager of a local bar came to me to gauge my opinion on why his successful establishment had gone from hero to zero even after a £500,000 refit. I told him that his design and his operational policies had meant that he was failing the elbow test, and that all his efforts and actions should be focused upon passing it. He looked bemused and said he had never thought about it in that way. Two months later, he closed. It was too late.

So what is the elbow test? Many bar owners believe that they are in the business of selling drinks and food. I disagree. They are in the business of creating an experience, and the really successful ones, like The Bubble Room, are providing something that people crave more and more. They want to interact with other people. In a world where most people are not even on speaking terms with their neighbours, there is a hunger for interaction with friends, acquaintances and most importantly strangers. Strangers add something of the unknown; they bring unpredictability, an excitement, an eccentricity, a different view of the world. Yet as a society we are fearful of strangers. We need a place of safety where we can comfortably encounter strangers and lose them just as easily if we need to. Bars which pass the elbow test provide the best environment for this. Where people are crammed together tightly in a space, they cannot help but bang elbows. The banging of elbows brings the proximity with strangers that we desire and the potential for interaction, however fleeting.

The Bubble Room is small and popular. It passes the elbow test very easily. That is what gives it the atmosphere that makes it a successful night time venue. It brings the flirtation with danger, real or perceived, and the possibility of a frisson of romance or sexual tension. You don't have to exchange longing glances with someone for weeks in The Bubble Room and then pluck up the courage to go over and speak to them. You have only to turn around and somebody will have banged your elbow.

The Bubble Room passes the elbow test better than anywhere in the village. It wasn't foreseen but it was with great joy that Lee tore up his business plan. He now understands the power of the elbow test.

'It's true. The amount of times when we have had a full restaurant and people have eaten then stayed for a drink after their meal. We have a big crush in the bar and people move from the restaurant to the bar because they prefer the crush. We ask people if they would like to move to sit in the restaurant and people say ,"No, we would rather stand here".'

A boy in a protective bubble?

Looking at the success of The Bubble Room today, it would be tempting for some to conclude that Lee Mason had it easy. He is from a respectable and stable family; mum and dad had complementary skills and loaned him the start-up capital; even his younger brother has taken a job behind the bar.

But don't forget, he was taking a risk. He was doing really well at work, yet gave up his job. He was taking on premises that had limitations and had been the scene of one failure after another. Importantly, he was doing it in the hands-on style that he has always preferred.

'We got the place. It was just me for two months from July until August. It was me, completely gutting the place. The previous owner left everything here, but we didn't want anything. I gave up my job; I'm on no pay, gutting the whole place; following my dad's design, my own ideas and some my mum threw in of her own. We worked as a team and I made it into a complete empty shell. It was tatty. The kitchen was greasy; the front had all sea grass carpets and big red panels, sockets in the walls that didn't work. The bar was misshaped. We ripped the plaster off the walls and we exposed the beams to get an industrial effect.'

Then he took on his right-hand man, Chris Carsons. They had worked to-gether at Mottram Hall, and even though Chris had left long before Lee, they had remained good friends. Chris pitched in and they worked hand-in-hand with the builders on every aspect of the refit. Lee is the first to admit that his close relation-ship with Chris has been one of the keys to the success of The Bubble Room. He says:

'I knew I could trust Chris and knew what he was capable of. His cus-tomer service is spot on. He's brilliant and I can't fault him. I offered him the job as assistant manager to help run the day-to-day operation.'

They work well together because they have established a policy of frank and frequent communication.

'We are not at each other's throats, and we are not afraid to back down if we are wrong. Communication is something we try to instil into every member of staff. Me and Chris do that really well. If I'm not happy with something he's done I tell him and, likewise, Chris is the same with me. We will all talk about it and get through it rather than holding grudges.'

There has been an impressive work ethic driving the business even before it opened, and Chris will often work ninety hours a week as well as Lee.

So this is not some privileged boy in a protective bubble. He has taken risks, applied his experience, and used all of the strengths and skills of his team and support network. Nobody can be in any doubt he has and continues to work very hard.

Rarer than vintage Cristal

Lee's original business plan envisaged a 60:40 split in favour of food over drinks. It was originally envisaged that it would major as a restaurant. Passing the elbow test very early on, put paid to those ideas and the split is now more like 70:30 in favour of drinks over food.

You might think that that would make for a less profitable scenario, but then you have to remember that this is Alderley Edge. The name of The Bubble Room came about because the local Victoria Wine off-licence is well known for being the branch that sells more bottles of champagne than any other branch in the country. Lee themed the concept around champagne bubbles.

So it is perhaps not surprising that champagne, rather than pints of bitter, is the order of the day in The Bubble Room. Lee says:

'We do champagne from the standard all the way to the vintages. The most expensive bottle we have is a 1999 Cristal Rose Magnum, which is £1200. There are only two bottles in the whole of the North West of England, the other one my suppliers have. It's very, very rare. We keep it nice and subtle, we don't go shouting about it, we want somebody to be able to enjoy it.'

Lee and Chris were invited to Chez Louis Roederer, the home of Cristal champagne, where they toured the wine cellars and had dinner in the chateau. Since then, Louis Roeder has become their house champagne. This tiny little bar is getting through 3500 bottles of champagne every year.

Remarkably, Lee sells the 'standard' Cristal champagne for £190 a bottle, when elsewhere in the village it is £250. I am bemused by this, but he says simply, 'We don't want to rip people off'. If you want to step up a notch, a standard bottle of Cristal Rose 1999 goes for £350.

What could be rarer than vintage Rose Cristal champagne? Perhaps there is only one thing rarer than that – somebody who buys four bottles at a time. You will even find a customer such as this in The Bubble Room. Lee smiles as he thinks of her.

'She's had four bottles. She has fallen in love with Cristal. She just loves it. She has friends in France that can't get this champagne because it is so rare. She's bought four and has had two. There are two which we reserve for her here at just the right temperature. She can take it home or drink it here. We stock it for her – it's that extra customer service.'

Customer service is always at the front of his mind, and he has learned to adapt and evolve the business based on customers' comments – which shows remarkable tolerance because, I have noticed, in Alderley Edge, everyone wants to tell you how to run your bar. He reflects on this.

'Everyone knows how to run your business. We get this everyday; all day. I listen to what they've got to say because at the end of the day they know some things – some people you just have to be polite to; others can give you good ideas. We've had quite a few good ideas from people.'

150

In this way, they changed to a weaker beer so that drivers could feel more comfortable if they had a drink; changed from an a-la-carte menu in the restaurant to an all-day menu in both bar and restaurant; and introduced live music on Sunday nights. He likes it when he can adopt a suggestion.

'It also makes the person who suggested it feel like they are being listened to. That's good, that.'

For some though, the weaker beer is irrelevant. Bubble Room staff constantly have to get out the Windowlene to clean the mirror which stands at one end of the bar. Lee says:

'People walk straight into that mirror. Some people have done it more than once. They walk towards it full of power. The staff have to keep wiping forehead marks off the mirror. One guy, I don't think he was drunk either, was having a conversation with himself in the mirror and started shouting at it. He got hold of me and said, "There's somebody kicking off over there", and he took me and pointed into the mirror. He was politely asked to leave.'

He is pleased that The Bubble Room morphs into a different kind of venue as the day progresses. There are the breakfasters, especially at the weekends; followed by the ladies that lunch; early doors tends to be businessmen on their way home; and then diners and revellers in the evening. They try to maintain a relaxed ambience during the evening. He says:

'We try to make people comfortable. It sounds really bad saying that we get the "right" people in, but we don't want big groups coming in drinking. You know, 20–25 year olds who are just going to be loud and drink beer. Nice people who sit and have a bottle of champagne, a nice chat and get on with everybody else around, that's what we aim for. People have said to us that Friday and Saturday nights are good because it's like going to a kind of house party where everybody knows each other. Which is exactly what we want it to be.'

On the business not in the business

There is no doubt that Lee has worked really hard to turn his first venture into a success and he deserves it. To really begin to develop a business though, there comes a time when you have to step back; to begin to work 'on' the business rather than 'in' the business. Most people find this a difficult transition, but Lee is in a good position to move on from here. His close working relationship with Chris and his emphasis on procedures, training and communication mean that the business runs perfectly well when he is not there.

This is good, because it means he now has a real opportunity. An opportunity to grow the Bubble Room brand, and he is thinking along these lines.

'The plan is to get another one, in the right location, another affluent area. The question is, will it be a small village like Alderley, or a town? Most likely it'll be in the same sort of place, a nice local community.'

He wants to grow the Bubble Room brand, but wants to keep it independent, perhaps developing a small chain. Having paid off his loan to mum and dad within a year, his prospects seem bright. After an amazing first year, like-for-like sales are up by 17%.

Not for the Bubbleboy, though, the champagne lifestyle. He is too busy working. He has only one little luxury in life: he has taken out a membership at Mottram Hall leisure club – hardly pushing the boat out. But there is more. This year he intends to take one holiday and spend one day at Chester Races.

His feet are well and truly planted on the ground. He will not be seduced by the champagne lifestyle that surrounds him. If Lee Mason can pull himself away to work on the business, rather than in the business, he can achieve great things.

Watch out. There will be more Bubble Rooms. Will they be as successful? There is no reason why they shouldn't be as long as he remembers one thing.

To pass the elbow test.

Entrepreneurial insights from the Bubbleboy

- Tap into talent. Lee got off to a flying start by tapping into and focusing all of the talent around him. Listening to his dad's experiences and adopting his designs; taking styling advice from his mum; getting Chris in to labour alongside the builders; putting his brother behind the bar; he even got his girlfriend to paint flowers on the outside hoarding whilst the renovation work was going on. If you can assemble and motivate a team to work around you, you can achieve a lot in a short space of time.

- Be flexible. Lee's original business model proved to be off the mark. It was based upon a restaurant with a subsidiary bar. The whole business model turned upside down. He was sensitive to this and, rather than trying to force through his original plans, he adapted very quickly to what customers wanted. In addition, he is receptive to customers' suggestions, introducing small improvements which respond to customer needs and make them feel a part of the place.

- Become independent of the business. Even though Lee works a ninety-hour week, the business could work perfectly well without him. He has strong procedures and processes, coupled with good management support, which means the business can work independently from him. This will allow him to move on to the next big thing very quickly and develop it, comfortable in the knowledge that his existing operation works. That is, if he can overcome the psychological barrier that many start-up enterprisers face – being able to make the transition from working 'in' the business to working 'on' the business.

- Sometimes it's not logical. Sometimes businesses are successful in the defiance of any logic. The elbow test, for example, is counter intuitive. One would imagine that a premium bar should offer space. The fact that it doesn't and that people cram together means that The Bubble Room is fulfilling a psychological and social need. There have been suggestions that Lee should remove the dividing wall between the bar and the restaurant to make more space. Logically, this sounds like a splendid suggestion. If I am right about the power of the elbow test though, it will only do one thing for the business. It will kill it.

13

The Thinker

'Look. I just want to do great things with great people.'

Then of course, there is me. The Thinker. I earn my living by being able to think about things, something that has annoyed my children for years. It means that I don't have a proper job or even a job title. They feel embarrassed when their friends at school ask them what their dad does for a living.

'Dad, why can't you just be a postman or a builder like everybody else's dad?' they ask.

I can't, because on a day when I reached my lowest ebb, I made it my mission in life to do 'great things with great people'. That's all. I set out to earn a living by doing what I love.

I love to think about how things work, have ideas and then act upon them. I love to work with people who are cleverer, more talented or more inventive than me. I love to pursue and fix issues that I can be passionate about. Who would have thought that you could make a great living and have a fantastic life just by doing that?

And it all began, one day, in my little town, when a shy, imaginative boy was taken by his mum to the market.

Barmy Mick

The old Salford market was like a scene from a Lowry landscape. Monochrome figures stooped over, battling against a chill wind and constant drizzle under a slate grey sky.

Barmy Mick always stole the show. He was a showman masquerading as a market trader or a market trader masquerading as a showman, I'm not sure which. Either way, he was good at his business, the business of selling crockery to people who faced a constant struggle to put food on the table.

Always, there was a huge excitable crowd around Barmy Mick's stall. He wore a diamond effect tiara, matching earrings and a pearl necklace. It was pure show-biz. He would take a thirty-two piece tea set, whip the crowd up into a frenzy, and following a theatrical pause, he would hurl all thirty-two pieces high into the air. There were gasps. People put their hands over their ears waiting for the calamitous crash of crockery. Yet Barmy Mick was not as Barmy as he looked. He always made the catch.

This might not sound much now, but when you are eight years old and only two TV channels exist, this was pure magic. It was an unforgettable moment. It was the prelude to one of those small, seemingly insignificant events that end up influencing the whole course and direction of your life.

My mum pointed to the stall next to Barmy Mick's. It was scruffy, piled high with dog-eared, second-hand books. She gave me sixpence and gave me an instruction which I obeyed: 'Go and choose any book that you like'. There were no trumpets, heralding angels or flashing lights to let me know that this was to be a significant moment. In retrospect, I can now see that it was.

I could have chosen any book. I know exactly which book I did choose all those years ago, because as I look across my office today, I can see it. I use it all the time. For the past fifteen years it has been a centrepiece of some of my talks, workshops and seminars. When I look at the work that has flowed towards me as a result, it can be valued at half a million pounds and it still keeps coming. That's not a bad return for sixpence.

That's not the only return I have had. This book has helped me to shape my values, beliefs and principles. It has allowed me to experience the power of metaphor as a tool for dealing with some of my most difficult problems and to create some unbelievable opportunities. It saved me when I was at my lowest ebb, it helped me to develop an idea which is transforming the lives of hundreds of young men and which has the potential to spread around the world.

It has helped me to move from the poorest square mile in Britain to the richest. Not that wealth itself is necessarily the defining thing; it is the distance travelled that is important – intellectually, emotionally and aspirationally. It has helped me appreciate that thinking about things, noticing what's important and acting upon them can take you a long, long way.

Today, I live a life that I can love, to the point that I often have to remind myself that it is happening, it is true and I am not imagining it.

You may be wondering to yourself why you are reading *To the Edge*, when you really should be rushing out to buy a copy of the book that I bought from a scruffy stall next door to Barmy Mick's.

Well, were you to look for a copy, you would be very unlikely to find one. It was first published in 1949, and though rare today, it would probably have little value to anyone other than me. You will be surprised when I tell you the title is *Teach Yourself Soccer*. Written by FNS Creek, who played for Corinthian Casuals and England. It is really a rudimentary instruction manual, designed to develop basic skills.

But it illustrates an important principle, one which allows me to earn a living by thinking about things. The idea is not so much *what* information you take into your head, or even *how much* information you are able to absorb. It is what you do with it, how you think about it, how you connect seemingly disparate pieces of information together, how you imagine, visualize and act.

When you are a shy, skinny kid growing up in one of Britain's toughest neighbourhoods, you need to develop something. You need to find self-belief, self-confidence, leadership, tenacity, humility, a will to win, a sense of fair play and an ability to create something out of nothing. Those are just some of the things that this book taught me. It is a good thing it did because, just as Stewart Pickering observed in Chapter Eight, the educational system conditioned us to fail.

When you are a shy, skinny kid in a tough neighbourhood, there is no hiding place. The method of choosing teams for the daily street soccer match was to line everyone up against the wall, and two people would take alternate picks. Guess who got picked last?

Things changed when I got my book, and when I look back I can understand why. I put in the time practising the drills in the book alone. When the teams were picked, I found myself moving along the wall, until one day I became the picker. The effect of that on my self-belief was startling. I probably wasn't a much better player than before, but I began to believe I was. It taught me that if you become more positive, if you become passionate about something, it is contagious and other people will follow you. It also taught me that self-belief can take you a long way. It taught me how to win and how to lose.

Little by little, a shy, skinny kid learned to be a man because of a sixpenny book. Often, in difficult times, I've drawn on my experiences as a street soccer star, using the game as a metaphor for life, helping me to work out what to do next.

Like most kids, I had a hero. He was the Belfast Boy and his name was George Best. Way back in Chapter Five you will remember that the Hustler, Selwyn Demmy was pictured on holiday with George, and that photograph appeared in many newspapers in the week that George was laid to rest. If you think a little harder, you will remember that two photographs achieved prominence in the papers that week.

The second was taken in the spring of 1968. Three people came together for just a few minutes and then went their separate ways – the hero, the amateur photographer and the boy. The hero was soon to become the greatest footballer in the world. His name was George Best. The amateur photographer was taking his lunch break and he spotted a boy talking to his hero and captured the moment on film. His name was Sefton Samuels. Subsequently he became professional and exhibited in The National Portrait Gallery in London, with one of the images he photographed on that day, which also featured on Paul Weller's 1995 album Stanley Road. And the boy? Well, the boy was me.

I searched a lifetime for this picture. I never found it. When George was dying I told my children that I was convinced this picture existed, and it was my destiny to find it. They laughed and said that it was just another of my outlandish stories.

Some weeks later, on the very day that George was laid to rest, I opened the centrespread of the *Manchester Evening News*. There it was. This picture was spread across two pages and they wanted to know who the boy was. Since then I have become friends with the photographer, Sefton Samuels, and he has given me a signed copy of the photograph. This is also in front of me in my office, next to the book I bought from the market, reminders to me that, in this great future, you can't forget your past. Your past helps to orientate you and helps you to understand how far you have come. It also offers lessons, lessons for dealing with the opportunities and threats, the ups and the downs, in an increasingly chaotic world.

So, for me, it was a slow start. I've always been a late developer, but once I get going I'm very, very quick. I then found myself at a stage of my life which is hard to describe. I have heard a useful phrase to describe the feeling I had: 'the quickening'. It describes that phase when, suddenly, ideas, opportunities and possibilities are hurtling towards you at breakneck speed. When I went to bed at night I longed for the morning time, I just want this 'quickening' process to continue.

Boxed in

Nobody imagined I would do anything much with my life. My teachers even told me that. I was bright but disinterested so I left school at sixteen and went to work in a cardboard box factory. Then something just clicked. I became fascinated by all the different materials, the range of manufacturing methods and the mathematics of cardboard boxes in all their different forms. I couldn't get enough of it. I was a kid who struggled with sums at school, now I was capable of doing complex geometry and simultaneous equations. I became passionate about the whole thing, and when you are passionate, everything is easy. They put me in the buying office and sent me to night school.

One of the tutors began a course on something called economics. I'd never heard of it, but again, something clicked. I just got it. I would regularly score 100% on test papers. This tutor asked why I hadn't gone to university. I thought he was either winding me up or talking to someone else. He produced a university application form, filled it in with me and posted it.

My father went mad. The very idea of giving up a good job in a cardboard box factory to be a student was incomprehensible to him. Mum told him in no uncertain terms to leave me alone, and it was never mentioned again.

On the day I finished my finals, I took a walk to the cardboard box factory. It was closed. It was in liquidation. Had I stayed, I would have been heading for the dole. Instead I had a degree, and was heading – well, I wasn't sure where I was heading.

Click, click, click

I didn't realize it, but this 'quickening' was beginning to happen again. My first job on leaving university was in the National Health Service. I began at the very bottom of the management pyramid, Scale One. But something about it just clicked. Just seven years later I had reached Scale 32, one stop from the very top. But I was impatient and competitive. Even though I was young I felt I deserved the top job. They advised me to wait a little while. I couldn't.

One day, a professor came to try to sell us consultancy services. I thought they had some interesting theories, but it was clear to me that they were detached from the real world. They didn't understand the complex funding mechanisms which underlie public sector bodies; the multi-dimensional accountability structures; or the politicking that was necessary just to get things done.

Some days later I rang him and said that he would never get a piece of work from the NHS. He listened and asked me to come to lunch. After lunch he said, 'Why don't you get a proper job and come and work in the private sector?' This was an interesting idea. I wanted to be the best and the NHS was stalling me. He offered me a 25% pay rise, and this helped clinch the deal. I was to come and set up a Health Management consultancy, in Europe's largest university based consultancy business.

It sounded great. I was keen to learn all about being a management consultant. I remember my first day; I was so looking forward to my induction into the world of private sector business. The professor called me down to his office. Two minutes later I left his office, my induction period complete. In retrospect it was a short sentence which proved to be a defining moment in my career in business.

I looked eagerly across his executive desk. He welcomed me to the company. Then he simply held up a blank invoice and said, 'Malcolm. From now on you live by invoices. No invoices and you are dead.' That was it.

I went to my office with a totally new perspective on life. From now on, my most precious asset was time. In the NHS, people loved to complicate things. The minimum time for a meeting was one hour, and three to four hour meetings were not unusual. Each person that spoke seemed to feel that they had a duty to add an extra layer of complexity to whatever topic was under discussion. I couldn't afford this any more. 'No invoices and you are dead'.

I managed my time like gold dust. I had an insatiable work ethic anyway, so I doubled it. Meetings lasted ten minutes; we just decided what had to be done and did it.

I don't know why. Something just sort of clicked. I found that I had a remarkable aptitude for selling people things that they could not see or touch. Those intangible things like advice, consultancy and ideas. People began buying into me from all over the place, not just the NHS, but local authorities, airports, charities and private firms. After three years, I had gone from a desk, a telephone and a blank invoice to having the fastest growing, highest value, most profitable division in the whole group, and I took on two failing divisions and started another. My salary had doubled, but for some reason I still felt short-changed.

There were two people in my division who I worked closely with. Very bright and hungry, a bit different from the crowd. We would often eat together, and just for a laugh we set up a shell company with a view to one day going off and doing our own thing. We each invested the princely sum of £100.

It was agreed that I should choose the moment to break the news to the boss that sometime in the future we would be leaving. So I waited for the right time. We were in London and had just left a productive meeting. So as we walked to the tube, I began this conversation. It was meant to be non-threatening. I said we might go in a phased way, or somehow work in partnership with the company. I didn't get a chance to finish. The professor again delivered a single sentence which catapulted me into a different world. He stood absolutely still and stared me in the eyes. He simply said, 'It's war. Goodbye.' With that, he disappeared down into the tube station and we have barely uttered a word to each other since that day – now some twenty years ago.

The very next day, the three of us were asked to hand in our office keys and the alarm code was changed. The mortgage was due in three weeks and all we had was a shell company worth £300.

My brother had an office with two desks. We recruited our PA, so there were four of us sharing a borrowed desk and a single telephone. Our backs were against the wall, and as they say when the going gets tough, the tough get going. Boy did we get going. Three years later my income had doubled again. We had offices, staff, company cars, pension plans, and we had a business that was competing and winning against the big consultancy practices, even though we made it our policy never to trade on price.

We used to describe our approach as 'hungry'. An insatiable fire in the belly. All three of us felt it and when we were all on song we were just unbeatable. Yet money and success change things. When it was us against the world we pretty much ate, drank and almost slept together. Then, when we were successful and making money, we began to behave in odd ways. In that sense, there is something good about being hungry and poor and having your back against the wall. It creates an *esprit de corps.* In many ways, they were the best of times. Our troubles began when we'd made it. I would hear that Neil Sedaka song, 'Now looking through my tears, I miss the hungry years', and I would think, 'Yes. I know exactly what you mean, Neil'. Years later I was speaking at a conference with Tim Smitt, the man who created the Eden Project. He said, 'Try to create the spirit of war in times of peace'. It was the spirit of war that propelled us to success. When we began to lose it I found myself having to broker peace between my two partners whose lifestyles were diverging week by week. Instead of 'us against the world' it had become the two of them against each other, with me in the middle, trying hard to hold it all together.

After nine years, as a business we were still enjoying success, but for me the love for it had gone. I was successful on the outside, and dying on the inside.

I remember driving back from London one night. I'd been involved in leading a negotiation for the NHS against the private sector. The deal was, if I achieved nothing I could bill them nothing. That day I was able to bill them £25,000 for a single day's work, and that was ten years ago. Not a bad day's work really, but nobody celebrated the success, nobody said well done, and at 6a.m. the next morning I was at the airport waiting to get the plane to Aberdeen. For all the success, it was becoming an increasingly miserable existence.

Then I had a really simple insight which allowed me to glimpse a new kind of future. We thought we should get more exposure for our brand, so the idea was to put together a national conference. We could charge people to come whilst at the same time exposing ourselves as the experts in the field. I agreed that I would lead this. I put together a conference programme, bringing various experts together and we sent out the marketing material. I went on holiday for a week and returned to an unusually large amount of post on my desk. As I began opening the envelopes, I found booking form after booking form, cheque after cheque. People were signing up to come to this conference.

How could that happen? I had been lying on my back for a week and had made £20,000. Surely not. It started me thinking along a different track.

It got me thinking about Delia Smith.

Delia Smith not Adam Smith

Charles Leadbeater wrote a really interesting book called *Living on Thin Air*. It was about how the world was changing from a production-driven economy to a knowledge-based economy. The essence of it was that we are moving away from the economic principles laid down by the father of economics Adam Smith in the 18th century, and towards an economy where we have to look towards the likes of celebrity cook Delia Smith.

What Delia Smith does is package knowledge. It happens to be in the form of recipes. They are extremely well packaged and marketed. What this means is that Delia is able to make money whether or not she is in the kitchen showing you how to make a particular dish – which of course she can't be. She has taken her tacit knowledge and embedded it in a recipe. People all over the world can use the knowledge that Delia has embedded in the book at any time they want. As a consultant I was selling knowledge too, but it invariably depended upon me being there with the client. Not only was this exhausting – some weeks I had already worked the hours of a normal working week by Wednesday lunchtime, and I could be in Aberdeen one day and St Austell the next – it placed limits upon what could be achieved. There are only twenty-four hours in a day and 365 days in a year. As a consultant there is a limit to what you can earn.

What I realized was that the £20,000 had appeared on my desk whilst I was on holiday because I had behaved exactly like Delia Smith. I had created a recipe that people could buy into regardless of whether I was awake or asleep, whether I was in the office or in Australia. I thought that I should think about this a bit more.

I did. I was professionally unhappy and I was starting to see a glimmer of something, so I gave my partners a year's notice that I was cashing out. It was getting towards the end of that year when reality really hit me. I'd been so focused on trying to please everybody – my clients, my staff, my partners, my family – I hadn't realized that I was trying to do the impossible. My wife, trying to bring up a young family in the middle of nowhere, had noticed this. I had fallen out of love with my business. She had fallen out of love with me. My marriage was over.

I'd come a long way. I should have been at the height of my powers. Instead, there I was with no job, no home, no wife, separate from my children, and facing the inevitable divorce settlement.

These were the worst of times. Yet in a strange sort of way it brought back a feeling that I had had before. It was like the time when the boss said, 'No invoices and you are dead'. It reminded me of the day he said, 'It's war. Goodbye.' I was in one of those situations again. It was me against the world and everything was at stake.

I had to create the spirit of war in times of peace. So I did what any sensible person would do – I bought a beat up old caravan and put it in a farmer's field through the winter with no bathroom – moved in, and began to think my way out of this situation.

Great things with great people

People have asked me why I chose to do that – live in a caravan through a freezing winter. I didn't really have to. Looking back, I think it was about distancing myself from the material world. I was a very driven person, but I wasn't really driven by the money; I rarely had time to enjoy it. For that matter, I never really gave myself permission to enjoy it. There was always another mountain that needed climbing first. By distancing myself I was able to think about what was important to me and it allowed me to think completely differently.

I had a blank sheet of paper, literally and metaphorically. I set it down on the table. When I knew what I was going to do with my life I would write it down on that piece of paper. The paper remained blank for quite some weeks. I sifted through a lot of thoughts. I reviewed images in my mind. I remembered times when I had felt successful, fulfilled, really alive.

Then I asked myself a question: 'Malcolm. What do you really want to do with your life?' The answer came back. 'Look. I just want to do great things with great people.' I said it out loud just to see how it felt. I liked it. The piece of paper was no longer blank.

But how then, do you make a living from a nice idea like that? The answer was lying in the back of my mind. I simply had to think more like Delia Smith than Adam Smith. It was the perfect coming together of a cause that I could get really passionate about, and a means of doing it that was really going to stretch my intellect. The situation was do or die, me against the world – the place where I operate at my best.

Small insights can have a big effect. People are often so busy looking for the next big idea, they don't even notice the small insights. Many of the entrepreneurs in this book have been successful by noticing and acting on small things. In my business, I used to say to my colleagues, 'If you hear something three times in quick succession, there is probably an opportunity there.' So often that has proven to be correct.

That's how I got off the ground doing great things with great people. I noticed something that nobody else seemed to notice – and then I had it reinforced three times in quick succession.

I was invited to the opening of the London offices of a new body set up to distribute National Lottery Money. There was nothing much to see, it was just an office. Chris Smith, a Minister in the Department for Culture, Media and Sport gave a little speech. Whilst he was talking, I picked up a little prospectus about this new funding body. It was about twenty pages long, detailing all of the programmes they were funding. On page twenty, there was a very small paragraph. It concerned a new fund and they were intending to give out £125 million. I had never heard of this fund. Thinking I was out of touch, I turned to the person next to me. He had never heard of it either. Applying my 'rule of three', I asked two other people and neither had they. There was £125 million up for grabs and nobody seemed to know. Time to think like Delia.

Very quickly I put together a recipe. A recipe in the form of a conference that would tell people about this fund and how to get a slice of £125 million. It was a one day event and I charged people to come. For that day I earned £52,000.

I didn't write a business plan. I simply visualized situations which would represent success. I looked at pictures in my head. Over the years, all of those pictures and much, much, more have happened. I concentrate on doing great things with great people, and money just seems to follow almost as a by-product.

So over the years I've done all sorts of things with amazing, fantastic, intelligent, creative, passionate people. Radio Four's *Changing Places* did a programme about my idea to transform stadia into multi-use community assets. Instead of using stadia once a fortnight for sporting events, why not use them 365 days a year as places for health, education, enterprise and social cohesion – something which was groundbreaking at the time and is now quite common. I gathered together the movers and shakers who made New York City smoke free and fronted an all day live broadcast from New York into Liverpool to encourage the smoke free lobby in the UK. I played my small part in moving forward the smoke free legislation. I've written numerous books and think tank publications – they make money whilst you are asleep; I've got the government thinking about the link between criminal behaviour and entrepreneurial behaviour. They have the same characteristics, one goes one way and becomes a villain; the other goes another way and becomes a hero. It's time we identified criminal entrepreneurs early and channelled their undoubted abilities in a more positive direction;

Of course we all need human interaction, and I am able to get this as an international speaker; I've been working over four years on a programme called *Think like an eight year old*, designed to help sporting organizations think more creatively about how to get people more physically active. As a result I have visited more sport and physical activity projects than almost anyone in the world – 110 in one year alone; and I established a subscription publication which went into profit after just three months, when the usual time to profitability is 18 months. These are just some of the things that I have done by focusing on great things and great people. Money follows ideas in the world of Delia Smith.

Then, of course, I want to change the world. Even if it is only in a small way, I want to create an epitaph. My chance came in a very strange way. I was standing in Norton Barrie menswear shop in Wilmslow, funnily enough, almost opposite

Karl Massey's inspirational Cottrills store. I had a tie in one hand and my credit card in the other and I was in a hurry. My mobile rang and I suppose I should have ignored it. I am so glad I didn't.

It was a man called Giles Gibbons. He said, 'Look, you probably don't even remember me, but we met about a year ago in London. You had some interesting ideas, and I'm looking for an idea.' I was still trying to juggle a tie, a credit card and a phone; almost irritably I asked, 'Well, what kind of idea?' He said he was doing some work for a Foundation called Laureus. They were interested in sport tackling social issues. My mind began to whirl. I saw in my head a picture that I had ripped out of the *Guardian* newspaper a few weeks earlier. It was *The Scream* by Edvard Munch, and it accompanied an article on depression, and in particular how young men were most at risk.

So by then I was really in a hurry. I said to him:

'Social issues? You want social issues? Well look, 7000 people commit suicide every year, most are suffering from a treatable illness. It's called depression. One in three people will have it at some time in their lives. It's an epidemic which costs the NHS £340 million a year in drugs alone, and young men are most at risk. The NHS can't get to them, they won't go to the doctors – so why doesn't our national game do something about that?'

There was quite a long silence. Only much later did I understand why. Giles ended the silence. He quietly said, 'That's a brilliant idea. If you could put something on a piece of A4 paper I could get you $100,000 a year to try to do something.' You don't get an offer like that every day, and it sounded too good to be true, so I politely said that I would try to find some time to do that. Some time later, I understood the reason for the long silence. Giles' brother had tragically committed suicide two years earlier – suffering from depression.

I was just too busy to even think about writing something on a piece of A4 paper. That is, until the 'rule of three' kicked in again. I rarely watch television, and just two days after speaking to Giles I was at home in the daytime, with the TV on. There was a programme about how Monaco was home to many award ceremonies, including the sporting equivalent of the Oscars, the Laureus Sport for Good Awards. There was Catherine Zeta Jones, Michael Douglas, Ronaldo, Boris Becker and a host of stars. Something was telling me that this meant something to me, but I couldn't put my finger on it. Then it hit me: '"Laureus" – that was the word that the guy on the phone said the other day.'

But I was busy. Three days later I was in London preparing for an event involving 50 of Europe's top business leaders. At the bar, I overheard a foreign gentleman saying that he was attending the event, so I went over and introduced myself.

He did likewise. 'Delighted to meet you, my name is Michael Nobel, I'm from Sweden'. I laughed, 'Ha, ha, Nobel, Sweden. Like the Nobel Prize?' He didn't laugh; he just said, 'Yes. I'm one of those Nobels. I'm the Chairman of the Nobel Family Foundation. I'm waiting here to meet my friend Johan Koss, the speedskater. He won five gold medals at the Olympics and I presented him with an award along with Prince Albert in Monaco.'

Hold on, I thought. There was something funny going on here. I asked, 'An award in Monaco? Was it a Laureus award?' He smiled. 'Yes, have you heard of Laureus?' My mind was whirling again. I said yes, and above my head you can imagine a little 'think bubble' appeared, saying 'Yes ... three times'. It was happening yet again: the 'rule of three'.

I went home and wrote something down. It went something like this. If young men are most at risk of suicide, and they won't go to the doctors, where do they go? You see them every Saturday sitting in football grounds. Imagine if, when a man was depressed, instead of sending him to a doctor or a psychiatrist or giving him tablets, you sent him to a football stadium. Imagine if, instead of focusing on the negative, debilitating aspects of depression, you concentrated just on 'being the best you can be'. I thought about the way I had used football as a metaphor to help me think about and deal with situations, ever since I bought that book from the stall next to Barmy Mick's as a boy. I devised an eleven-week programme which always began with them talking about a footballing issue, and then switching it to equip them with tactics and techniques to deal with the issues in their life which were causing the depression. For example, session one is about goals. So the men begin talking about great goals they have seen. How managers set goals for their teams – clean sheets, get to the play-offs, 20 goals from midfield – and then we ask them what goals they have in their life. A common theme that has emerged is that men who suffer from depression often have never thought about or had any personal goals. So they set some goals, and over the following eleven weeks they learn tactics and techniques for taking more control over their lives, just by talking about football. We call the programme *It's a Goal!* After three years, this is no longer an interesting theory. We have a substantial body of evidence to show that it works. The results have been phenomenal.

I took on a psychiatric nurse to run the programme; his name is Pete Sayers and he must take the credit for making my idea work. He doesn't tell anyone his background, unless they ask. He wears a tracksuit and calls himself a coach. We like to keep it non-clinical and make it as different from an NHS experience as it could possibly be. We like to adopt an entrepreneurial approach, which Pete struggled with at first, having spent a lifetime in the NHS. Now he loves the freedom to take some chances, to try new things, to do things without having to form an over-arching strategy group. Our attitude is, 'If you see a snake, kill it. Don't set up a committee to consider the dangers of snakes'.

In responding to 'the rule of three', the Laureus Sport for Good Foundation has now given me over £250,000. We began in the smallest professional football club in England, Macclesfield Town, and then opened up a programme in the biggest club in the world, Manchester United. I've now created a social franchise, and as I write, I've sold the first one to Plymouth Primary Care Trust which intends to open up at Plymouth Argyle. There is a football stadium in every town and city in the world. Why shouldn't *It's a Goal!* spread around the world? That would be a nice epitaph.

This is a great example of what we need to encourage entrepreneurs to do: to apply their quirky, unusual ways of looking at the world, their extraordinary beliefs and behaviours, towards finding innovative ways to tackle social problems. It's what I did, because it was a great thing to do with great people. The spin-off has been that all sorts of business opportunities emerged indirectly. Laureus didn't just give me money. They have an academy comprised of forty-two of the world's greatest living sporting legends. They sent a few of them to help me. They have been fantastic in the support they have given to me. Their names are Sir Bobby Charlton, Sir Ian Botham and Dame Tanni Grey-Thompson, the greatest ever paralympic athlete.

What was it I wrote on that blank piece of paper? Great things with great people.

Yes.

Now … to the edge

It's been an amazing seven years since I took a simple yet momentous decision just to do great things with great people. I do believe in seven year cycles; it is nature's number after all. A seven year cycle is the natural time to move on, and I'm ready to do that.

I've been absolutely inspired by the people I have spoken to whilst writing this book. It has been a great education, too. A masterclass at Harvard Business School, if you like, over a few cups of coffee, the odd pint of Guinness, and the occasional glass of champagne.

I've laid down some great foundations. They have been built upon a passion for doing great things with great people – and the things I've learned by looking closely at Delia Smith.

Yet I feel that I am underachieving. It is time now to scale up these ideas. It is time once again to create the spirit of war in a time of peace.

It is time.

I am ready to get closer.

Closer to the edge.

Entrepreneurial insights from the Thinker

- Take notice of the 'rule of three'. I've lost count of the number of times I have done this in my business life and watched as it has led me towards great things. When you hear something three times in quick succession, the chances are that there is a business opportunity there. To do this, you must do something that people seem to find it harder and harder to do: you must shut up and listen. When I say listen, I don't just mean 'hear'; I mean actively listen. Get engaged in what people are telling you. However mundane it may seem, try to put yourself into the story that they are unfolding, try to feel the emotions involved. That way, the mundane can become magical. You can take pleasure in absorbing massive amounts of information, and in amongst it all you may just stumble across the 'rule of three'. One thing is for sure; if you are talking all the time, you will never benefit from the rule of three.

- Visualize. Images are the natural language of the mind and they are a great way to inspire yourself, create dreams and formulate goals. Play with images in your mind. Plans and key performance indicators are useful, but they will never set your heart on fire. Use KPIs as a compass to help you to work out if you are going in the direction of your dreams. After all when Martin Luther King took to the steps of the Lincoln Memorial in Washington DC on 28th August 1963, he didn't say, 'I have a strategic plan', did he? He had a dream. Have yourself a dream. Visualize.

- Create the spirit of war in times of peace. It is really easy to become complacent, especially if you have had an initial success. Complacency is not something that you will have encountered in any one of the stories in this book. If you are doing well, scare yourself a bit more. Try new things, take some bigger risks. It will bring out the best in you.

- Create an epitaph. If you want your epitaph to be 'He/she made a fortune' then perhaps you should go away and take a look at yourself in the mirror for a while. Go away and think about the true meaning of being human. I have no problems with people who make fortunes. I admire them, and I hope that you are inspired by the insights in this book to go and make one for yourself. But do realize your true potential. Entrepreneurs, with their quirky way of looking at the world and their extraordinary behaviours and beliefs, can do more than politicians to change the world we live in. They can do great things. Why not go and do great things with great people that can really make a difference? Get yourself a fitting epitaph – no amount of money will buy you one.

Appendix One

To the Edge Quick Quiz

Have you got the mind of a millionaire?

To the Edge: Personal Enterprise Quiz

Dr Adrian Atkinson is a business psychologist and Managing Director of Human Factors International. Over the past 25 years his work with entrepreneurs and wealth creators has enabled him to develop the Personal Enterprise Profile. This identifies the characteristics of people who are likely to be successful Wealth Creators and in particular the personality, intellectual ability and values that they show.

The following questionnaire is a brief version of the full questionnaire and offers an insight into your route to Wealth Creation. You can also complete the full version by going to www.humanfactors.co.uk

For each of the following five groups of statements choose the one statement which best describes the behaviour which would form the basis of your approach to starting your business.

Group 1	Working with other like-minded individuals	A
	Making a big effort to get the company structure right	B
	Willing to work seven days a week	C
	Realizing that technical excellence is the key to success	D
Group 2	Getting some qualifications before starting your own business	E
	Only starting the business with all the finance in place	F
	Keeping your existing job until your new business is established	G
	Seeing work as relaxation	H
Group 3	Making sure you have a social life as well and rarely work on the weekends	I
	Be willing to sell your house and car to start your business	J
	Taking your time to make all important decisions	K
	Plan your exit strategy from the beginning	L
Group 4	Not selling more than the company can deliver	M
	Making sure the product and services are perfect before getting sales	N
	Be willing to fire people who perform badly	O
	Developing business plans in order to make strategic decisions	P
Group 5	Always involving colleagues in decisions	Q
	Only aiming for the highest quality	R
	Be willing to sacrifice family life to move the business forward	S
	Realizing that all that matters in business is making money	T

Scoring
- Score 4 points each if you chose C, H, J, O, S
- Score 3 points each if you chose A, E, L, P, T
- Score 2 points each if you chose B, F, K, M, Q
- Score 1 point each if you chose D, G, I, N, R

Add up your total score and find out below which type of Wealth Creator you are likely to be.

Depending on the statements that you selected, if you have the appropriate Personality, Intellectual ability and Values, then you are likely to be an Expert, Corporate, Enterpriser or Strongly Entrepreneurial Wealth Creator.

Score of 5–9 – Expert
Not so attracted by personal risk or by commercial challenge. Sees value in getting processes right and focuses on achieving high-quality work. Prefers functional role using their technical knowledge and expertise. Often develops new technologies, products or processes.

Score of 10–14 – Corporate
Interested in developing a business within a structured context. Achieves by energizing functions and groups in organizations. Willing to take business risks rather than personal risks. Looks for business challenges within medium to large organizations.

Score of 15–18 – Enterpriser
Seeks excitement from making things happen. Finds personal risk-taking exciting but prefers to share risks and rewards with others. Focuses energy on achieving goals but maintains reasonable work/leisure balance. Dislikes routine and constantly seeks challenges which stretch them.

Score of 19–20 – Strongly Entrepreneurial
Enjoys starting own businesses and devotes all energy and time to make things happen, often at the expense of family, possessions and reputation. Restless and often dissatisfied with what they have achieved but very resilient and able to pick themselves up and start again. Sees work as relaxation and dislikes weekends and holidays.

Index

To The Edge

To The Edge

Entrepreneurial Secrets from Britain's Richest Square Mile

Malcolm McClean

CAPSTONE

First published 2007 by
Capstone Publishing Ltd. (a Wiley Company)
The Atrium, Southern Gate, Chichester, PO19 8SQ, UK.
www.wileyeurope.com
Email (for orders and customer service enquiries): cs-books@wiley.co.uk
The right of Malcolm McClean to be identified as the author of this book has been asserted in accordance with the Copyright, Designs
and Patents Act 1988

Other Wiley Editorial Offices: Hoboken, San Fransisco, Weinheim, Australia, Singapore and Canada.
Wiley also publishes its books in a variety of electronic formats. Some content that appears in print may not be available in electronic
books.
Library of Congress Cataloging-in-Publication Data
McClean, Malcolm .
To The Edge: Entrepreneurial secrets from Britain's richest square mile / Malcolm McClean.
   p. cm.
 Includes index.
 ISBN 978–1–84–112782–8 (pbk. : alk. paper)
PS3602.U733L54   2007
 813'.6—dc22   2006041314

ISBN   978–1–84–112782–8

Anniversary Logo Design: Richard J Pacifico

Typeset by Sparks in 11 pt Dutch (www.sparks.co.uk)
Printed and bound in Great Britain by TJ International Ltd, Padstow, Cornwall